There is a wealth of careful Bible
experience in this thoroughly usef
Christopher Ash, Director of the Proc
Training Course

Full of biblical wisdom, each chapter applies the gospel to the
heart issues of Christian living in today's world. Illuminating
our attitudes and challenging our motives, this clear and easy-
to-read guide is a tonic towards spiritual progress and fulfilment.
I warmly commend it.
David Jackman, Past President, the Proclamation Trust

All too often our Christian life falls into a mere dutiful obedience
to God that consists of outward conformity with little inner
reality. Graham Beynon is a wise and faithful guide who
challenges us to develop the right 'heart attitudes' to God. He
defines these attitudes clearly and biblically, and then shows how
to foster them practically by applying the gospel to every area of
our lives. You won't be able to read this book without being
changed and encouraged to live more wholeheartedly for God.
Highly recommended for anyone looking to deepen, guard,
transform or renew their spiritual life.
John Stevens, National Director, Fellowship of Independent Evangelical
Churches

This is a treasure of a book for those who wish to take their
Christianity seriously and see real change in their lives through
a deeper knowledge of God, the gospel and themselves. It is
warmly written, winsome in application, and clear and
comprehensive in its treatment of the human heart as the Bible
sees it. Here we have heavenly truths applied in a down-to-earth
way. This is a book which is of value for Christians and non-
Christians alike and is to be enthusiastically commended.
Melvin Tinker, Senior Minister, St John, Newland, and author

HEART
ATTITUDES

ivp

HEART
ATTITUDES

CULTIVATING LIFE
ON THE INSIDE

GRAHAM
BEYNON

INTER-VARSITY PRESS
Norton Street, Nottingham NG7 3HR England
Email: ivp@ivpbooks.com
Website: www.ivpbooks.com

British Library Cataloguing in Publication Data
A catalogue record for this book is available from the British Library.

ISBN: 978–1–78359–171–8

Set in Dante 12/15pt
Typeset in Great Britain by CRB Associates, Potterhanworth, Lincolnshire
Printed in Great Britain by Ashford Colour Press Ltd, Gosport, Hampshire

*Inter-Varsity Press publishes Christian books that are true to the Bible and that
communicate the gospel, develop discipleship and strengthen the church for its
mission in the world.*

*Inter-Varsity Press is closely linked with the Universities and Colleges Christian
Fellowship, a student movement connecting Christian Unions in universities and
colleges throughout Great Britain, and a member movement of the International
Fellowship of Evangelical Students. Website: www.uccf.org.uk*

To Nige, my twin brother, whom I love and respect.
Your life is an example to me.

acknowledgments

This book comes from a series of sermons preached at two different churches (Avenue Community Church, Leicester and Grace Church, Cambridge) and elsewhere. Thanks are owed to all those who kindly gave constructive feedback and improved the material as a result.

I'm also grateful to my wife, Charis, for reading some of the early chapters and the enriching discussions that followed. Eleanor Trotter, my editor, has tightened my writing as usual, particularly giving her gentle prompts on what needed to be pruned. Lastly, Lucy Langley read the manuscript and helped sharpen the shape of the final version. Above all, I acknowledge God and his great goodness.

contents

introduction: welcome to heart surgery

Let me tell you about three people I know.

Jim was very involved in his local church, part of the leadership team and in charge of a small group. He was serving well and working hard. One day I got a phone call from Jim's anxious wife. 'Please speak to him,' she said. Jim had crashed very badly spiritually. He still hasn't really recovered.

We have spoken at length over what happened. There were lots of things going on, but one key element he brought out was this: 'Christian life has become something I *do*, not something I *feel*.' It had become outward behaviour with no heart behind it. Jim would happily have signed up to any decent doctrine – there was no heresy involved, and there was no overt disobedience in his life. But there was no heartbeat any more.

Clare is pressing on as a Christian. She reads her Bible every day and teaches regularly in the Sunday school. But there is no enthusiasm in it. It is, by her own admission, dry duty. I was speaking to her a while ago and asked about her walk with God. Her expression was gloomy. 'Nothing about God or the gospel grips me any more,' she said. As a result, her heart isn't really in it these days.

Bill and I have been meeting up for a while. We've discussed all sorts of issues – anxiety, depression, marriage and work. But just recently, as we talked more, I asked how he was feeling towards God. The lovely thing about Bill is that he doesn't pretend and doesn't try to give the 'right' answer. So, true to form, he said simply, 'I feel angry with him.' He went on to talk about how he felt God hadn't treated him fairly, hadn't given him what he'd asked for, and so he felt bitter.

This book looks at key heart attitudes. We all know that our Christian life involves what we believe: truth about God, ourselves, salvation, the future, and more. We also know that it involves how we live: what God asks of us, living for his glory, life together as his people in the church, and more. But the Christian life also involves what is going on inside us: our motivations, desires and feelings. God is concerned that we know the truth, and that we obey him, but he's also concerned about our hearts.

Who we are, not just what we know

The New Testament is full of teaching and instruction so that we know what is true. Consider Paul's letter to the church in Rome. He spends many chapters explaining sin and justification, union with Jesus and adoption, the place of Israel, and the future. There can be no doubt: he wants people to understand the truth. In fact, he explicitly warns about those who are zealous for God, but whose zeal is not based on right knowledge (Romans 10:2). So we must not shy away from thinking hard. We must be eager to learn more about God and his plans, and so it is essential that we understand

God's Word. After all, Jesus said it was the truth that would set us free (John 8:32).

But God is deeply concerned with who we are, not just what we know. He is concerned with the impact his truth makes on us, not just with the fact that we can repeat it. In short, God wants his truth to *shape* us.

Who we are, not just what we do

In that same letter to the church in Rome, Paul describes how Christians should live. He describes how they should love each other, respond to persecution, obey their governments, handle differences of opinion and give themselves to supporting mission. God expects the lives of his people to look different from those who do not know him because of their faith.

But again, right actions are not enough. God is concerned with who we are, not just what we do, and why we do what we do, not just that we do the right thing. He wants his people to live differently because we are a *changed* people.

The centre of our lives: our hearts

In other words, God is concerned with our hearts. We tend to use the word 'heart' today to refer to our feelings, and, as we'll see below, feelings are indeed involved. But in the Bible, 'heart' is much deeper than just feelings. It refers to the centre of our lives. Proverbs tells us that all of our life flows from our hearts (Proverbs 4:23), and Jesus tell us that our words and actions flow from our hearts (Luke 6:45). Our hearts are about what we love and fear, what we desire and hope for, what we *really* believe. Our hearts are the engine which drives each one of our lives.

So, in his letter to Rome, Paul talks about 'heart attitudes'. He mentions God's love in our hearts, knowing peace with

God, enjoying hope for the future, assurance in the face of trials and joy in salvation.

I've used the phrase 'heart attitudes' for these areas, but really I almost want to use the word 'feelings'. The problem is that 'feelings' usually refers to emotions that come and go because of circumstances and events. What I have in mind here is something more constant. Yet it does have a 'feeling' component to it. When I am thankful, that will involve some feeling of gratitude. When I am at peace, I will not be feeling anxious. When I am joyful, there will be a smile on my face (even though there may also be reasons to cry and tears running down my cheeks).

Our hearts are the engine which drives each one of our lives.

In some ways this book is a follow-on from my book *Emotions*. There I explained the whole range of emotions: from fleeting feelings to ongoing moods, through to 'heart attitudes'. I argued that the 'heart attitude' end of the spectrum was far *more* than emotions, albeit with an emotional element to it. It is that end of the spectrum that we are looking at here. Heart attitudes are the 'orientation' of our hearts, our disposition, indeed almost our character. They have to do with who we are, our experience of God and our feelings towards him.

The missing hinge: our hearts

Heart attitudes can be the missing hinge of the Christian life. Without such attitudes, we know what to think and how to live, but we can struggle to connect the two. I may know that God has been kind to me in salvation, and I know I should live for him, but without any joy or gratitude, that will easily become grudging obedience. I may know that God is sovereign and cares for me, but without any experience of peace in my heart, my life remains driven by my worries.

In fact, without right heart attitudes, we face the danger of an external religion. We can know all the right answers, answer Bible study questions, spot a heresy a mile off and appreciate a good sermon. We also know what Christian behaviour looks like, what to do and what not to do, what to say and what not to say.

Heart attitudes can be the missing hinge of the Christian life.

But it can all be outward conformity, with little or no inner reality. I think of Jesus' words to the religious leaders of his day. They knew the Bible very well and believed it. They were very careful in their living for God. But, referring to them, Jesus quoted some chilling words from Isaiah:

> These people honour me with their lips,
>   but their hearts are far from me.
> They worship me in vain;
>   their teachings are merely human rules.
> (Mark 7:6–7)

That's the worst-case scenario: hearts that are far from God, even in people who still say the right things. But there can be lesser forms of the same problem. I think of Jesus' words to the church of Laodicea in Revelation. Those people believed the truth and seemed to be living for Jesus, but he said,

> Yet I hold this against you: You have forsaken the love you had at first.
> (Revelation 2:4)

That's the common theme in the cameos of Jim, Clare and Bill whom we met earlier. In different ways, and to different degrees, their Christian life had just become something they did, outward behaviour with little or no heart behind it. At worst, it had become a mask, and when we realize that it's no more than that, we may simply take the mask off.

Church culture doesn't always help us here either. We can be encouraged to play a part. We know what we expect each other to say and do. And some of that can be good and right, encouraging a helpful expectation of one another. But it can also reinforce mask wearing. It can be like putting on our metaphorical Sunday best, but covering over what's really going on in our hearts.

Isaac Watts, the famous hymn writer, knew how crucial this issue was, and the very real dangers of hypocrisy. He said,

> It is not enough for the eye to be lifted up to him, or the knee to bow before him; it is not enough for the tongue to speak of him, or the hand to act for his interest in the world; all this may be done by painted hypocrites whose religion is all disguise and vanity. But the heart with all the inward powers and passions must be devoted to him in the first place: This is religion indeed. The great God values not the service of men, if the heart not be in it.[1]

The gospel and heart surgery

So we need to go to work on our hearts. You could think of this book as open-heart surgery. Of course, only God can change our hearts, but he calls us to be involved in that process too. With God at work in us, we want to renew and change our attitudes. We want our hearts to be shaped differently.

The key surgical instrument in this operation is the gospel – the good news of Jesus Christ in his life, death, resurrection, ascension and return. It is this that should reshape and change us. The gospel creates, sustains and nurtures right heart attitudes. So, we're going to look at key heart attitudes and, in each case, think about how the gospel should bring it about.

One direction only

There's a caveat with this book that I should make clear. We're going to look in one direction only. That is, we're only going to consider heart attitudes towards God – looking upwards. So we'll think about fearing God, loving God, knowing God's peace, and much more. I need to point this out because the Bible is also full of heart attitudes that look horizontally towards others. We could think about loving each other, being compassionate and kind to one another, and more. But we won't. That's not because I don't think these things are important – I really do – but only that the vertical dimension offers plenty of scope and merits special attention. The horizontal is worth another book in itself.

So please join me in heart surgery. Yes, I know from experience that it can be painful. Thinking through the issues has revealed things about my own heart that I'd have preferred not to learn. But ultimately, the effect is healing. And I can also honestly say that thinking these things through has done me good! I do hope that you will find the same.

1
love

'Love God, and do what you will.'

So said Augustine, the famous early-church theologian. This sentence has been much quoted, and much misunderstood, ever since. Some have taken it to mean that as long as you love God, you can do whatever you like.

That would actually fit our culture today rather well. We want the freedom to love, but we also relish the idea of freedom. It's great to love someone, but I should still be able to do what I want too. Love shouldn't constrain me; it should leave me free. Applied to God, this means I can have warm feelings of love towards him, and then enjoy life on my own terms.

But that's not what Augustine meant.

He uses the illustration of a plant where everything flows from its root. It's an image Jesus himself used: our words and actions are the fruit which reveal what sort of root we have (Luke 6:43–45). So Augustine said, 'Let the root of love be within, of this root can nothing spring but what is good.'[1]

He means that if we love God, we can do what we want, because we will only want to do what is good. If we love God, then the attitude of our heart is focused on what God wants, and a right life will flow from this. It's like saying that if I truly love my wife, then I will only do what is loving towards her; or if I love my children, then I will only do what is good for them.

This is a wonderful picture of having a heart that loves God, which flows out into all that I do. This is the reason why God's people are told to love him with everything that they are:

> Hear, O Israel: the LORD our God, the LORD is one. Love the LORD your God with all your heart and with all your soul and with all your strength.
> (Deuteronomy 6:4–5)

When, in the New Testament, Jesus is asked about the greatest commandment, he turns back to this verse in Deuteronomy:

> 'The most important one,' answered Jesus, 'is this: "Hear, O Israel: The Lord our God, the Lord is one. Love the Lord your God with all your heart and with all your soul and with all your mind and with all your strength."'
> (Mark 12:29–30)

Moses, and then Jesus, tells us to love God with all of ourselves: our heart, our soul, our mind, our strength. This isn't trying to divide us into separate parts; it's saying that we are to love God with every part of our being, and with 'all' of every part.

Christians should be those who, above all else, have hearts which love God. If you do, then you can 'do what you will'.

For a life of love for God will inevitably flow from a heart that loves God above all else.

What does it mean to love God?

Love is one of those curious words that we use all the time, but it is tricky to define. The famous 'Love is . . .' cartoon series has produced daily one-line descriptions of love for over forty years. They range from soppy sentimentality: 'Love is when he's your sunshine', to sweet observations: 'Love is growing closer as the years go by', to significant insights: 'Love is making sacrifices'.

But most of the cartoons focus on feelings of romantic love, which reflects contemporary culture. And feelings of attraction are great, but we're usually

Love is surely a more solid thing than how I feel.

very aware that they don't convey all that 'love' can mean, even in a romantic relationship. Love is surely a more solid thing than how I feel.

When asked what it means to 'love' God, the standard response is: 'It's not just a feeling.' Or, 'It's not a feeling, it's an act of the will.' But what exactly is it, in addition to a feeling? Or what act of will is it? For such a commonly used word, it's difficult to verbalize.

Some examples can help us here though. When I got married, I promised to *love* my wife, not primarily to *feel* in love with her, but rather something closer to 'loyalty'. I was saying I would remain committed to her, although of course my feelings had to come into play too! So, staying loyally committed to my wife is great, but there should be devotion to her as well.

Or suppose we said someone 'loved' football. We'd be saying it was very important to them, and probably that they had some loyalty to a team. But again, they would have to feel something for the game. There would be passion as well as commitment.

As we shall see in a moment, those illustrations capture something of what loving God involves. This is how I like to sum it up: it is *devoted loyalty to him*. It has two parts to it: *devoted* loyalty, which includes my devotion or passion for him, and devoted *loyalty*, which includes my loyal obedience and constancy in living for him.

Loyalty

We see the 'loyalty' aspect immediately in Deuteronomy 6, for these verses following the call to love God describe a life of loyal commitment to him:

> These commandments that I give you today are to be on your hearts. Impress them on your children. Talk about them when you sit at home and when you walk along the road, when you lie down and when you get up. Tie them as symbols on your hands and bind them on your foreheads. Write them on the door-frames of your houses and on your gates.
> (Deuteronomy 6:6–9)

Love for God here is closely linked with his Word, because our love is expressed by obeying him. If we love God with all our hearts, then we will do what he says.

The result for the Israelites was that God's Word was to be on their hearts. They had to impress his commands on their children. God's Word had to be applied to all of life: sitting at home and walking down the road, lying down and getting up. The idea here is not simply talking about God's Word, but that it should shape all that the Israelites did.

This meant that they had to write God's commands around their house, because these were to affect how they lived as a family. The commands were also to be written and around their town – the 'gates' were the town gates where business would be conducted and community decisions made. So God's Word guided their public as well as their family life.

The command to love God is clearly talking about far more than a feeling. It is a heart orientation to God as the most important person in life, the one we live for, and consequently stay loyal to. It is God as the commanding officer you will always follow, the father you will never disobey, the spouse to whom you will remain utterly faithful.

We see this throughout the rest of Deuteronomy. Look at the following verses and see how love is always tied to loyal commitment and obedience:

Love the LORD your God and keep his requirements, his decrees, his laws and his commands always.
(Deuteronomy 11:1)

. . . to love the LORD your God, to walk in obedience to him and to hold fast to him . . .
(Deuteronomy 11:22)

. . . to love the LORD your God and to walk always in obedience to him . . .
(Deuteronomy 19:9)

. . . that you may love the LORD your God, listen to his voice, and hold fast to him.
(Deuteronomy 30:20)

Loving God means keeping his laws, walking in obedience.

It means 'holding fast to him', not being pulled away to anything else, but listening to him and obeying what he says.

This is why Jesus says, 'Whoever has my commands and keeps them is the one who loves me' (John 14:21), and 'Anyone who loves me will obey my teaching' (John 14:23).

I remember talking to a student called Liz about relationships: who she was going out with, what they were doing, and so on. She had come up to me after a talk I'd given on the subject. I guessed from the way she started talking that she was going to disagree with what I'd said earlier. But to my amazement, she agreed with me. She agreed that she and her boyfriend were doing something wrong, and that God disapproved. *OK, I thought, I judged that one wrongly. She agrees they're disobeying God, so now they'll stop.* But then came her amazing words: 'But I still really love God and that's what's important.'

Liz was separating her attitude to God from her living for God. But Moses' words and Jesus' words will not allow for that. Love for God has to be expressed in obedience to him. I had to say to her, 'I'm very sorry, but you don't love God.'

Love is shown in devoted *loyalty*.

Devotion

Loving God also involves devotion to him. This is different from outer conformity, for it would be possible to obey God's commands externally, but still have no love for him. In fact, I could 'do the right thing', but still have a heart that was cold or angry towards God.

Back in Deuteronomy 6, the original command is to love God with all of ourselves – all our heart, all our soul, all our strength. No part of us is excluded. I can't love God with my actions, but not in my mind. I can't love him with my words, but not in my heart. Our love must therefore include how we feel towards him.

Later in the Old Testament, the prophet Jeremiah describes how the nation of Israel was devoted to God after he rescued them from Egypt. God says through Jeremiah,

> I remember the devotion of your youth,
>   how as a bride you loved me
> and followed me through the wilderness,
>   through a land not sown.
> (Jeremiah 2:2)

You get the sense that God's people 'felt' something for him, don't you? They followed him in a devoted and close relationship. This is why God uses the picture of a bride: true love for God will include affection for him. Our hearts are warm towards him rather than cold.

We see an example of this need for devotion in Paul's words to the Corinthian church. He speaks about someone who acts for God, but who doesn't actually have any love:

> If I give all I possess to the poor and give over my body to
> hardship that I may boast, but do not have love, I gain nothing.
> (1 Corinthians 13:3)

In other words, the most self-sacrificial action can be done without love, without the right inner motivation. Without that heart desire, our obedience, and even our sacrifice, is worth nothing.

We saw something similar in the introduction. In the book of Revelation, Jesus writes letters to a number of churches about how they are doing. One church, Ephesus, is doing the right things: they are doctrinally sound, they have persevered and they have endured hardships. Unlike other churches being addressed, there's no mention of any disobedience. But, says

Jesus, 'I hold this against you: you have forsaken the love you had at first' (Revelation 2:4). It seems that their hearts had grown cold.

God wants loyal obedience, but he wants it from a heart that is devoted to him. I think this is unique among religions. Many of them talk about obeying their god. Most indeed have a list of commands to be obeyed. Many talk about fear of their god, and having awe and respect. But only Christianity talks about loving God.

Love for God includes *devotion* to him.

Why we love God

We've now explored what loving God means, but within this passage, we are also told why we should love God, even to remember why.

Firstly, we love God *because of who he is*. There is a crucial verse that comes just before that famous command to love God with all ourselves:

> Hear, O Israel: the LORD our God, the LORD is one. Love the
> LORD your God with all your heart . . .
> (Deuteronomy 6:4–5)

Jesus shows us how important this statement is, because when he's asked about the most important commandment, he doesn't simply quote the command to love God, but begins with these words about God being one (Mark 12:29).

The big question is: what does it mean that God is 'one'? Some take it to mean that God is unique. The Lord is our God and him *alone*. The argument is that he is the only true God, so you should love him with all your heart.

That's possible, but it's not actually what the words say. The word Jesus uses simply means 'one', not 'only'. The alternative, which I think is more likely, is that this is not so much about God's uniqueness, but more about his integrity. It's saying that the Lord is one in that he's not divided.

This is best illustrated by comparison with the gods of the nations around Israel. They were thought to be a fickle and changeable bunch. You weren't always sure what kind of mood they'd be in. That meant you would be wary in your interactions with them, not quite sure which side of them you'd meet today.

If someone is like that, the result is that you can't trust yourself to them. You don't give total loyalty to a boss who is unpredictable. And in a marriage, it's very hard to give yourself completely when you feel you can't trust the other person.

By comparison, God is saying, 'I am one', 'I'm not divided' and 'I have integrity'. This leads us to God's faithfulness, consistency and reliability. He won't become a different sort of God and surprise us. The more you ponder that, the more important it becomes. In his being and his purposes, God is one. It means

We love God because of who he is.

he keeps every promise. He is utterly reliable. He will never change.

So the logic is this: the Lord our God is one; he is utterly consistent and faithful; and so we can commit ourselves to him completely. We can love him with all that we are because he is so dependable.

This is important because there's a real challenge in being called to love God with all that we are. It's scary. It means handing your life over to someone else, putting them in charge. But we need to know and remember that God is the One we *can* do that with. We can, and must, trust ourselves to him because of his integrity and consistency. We can live in devoted loyalty to him.

We love God because of who he is.

Secondly, we love God *because of what he does.* Later verses in Deuteronomy 6 raise a question that will be asked further on:

> In the future, when your son asks you, 'What is the meaning of the stipulations, decrees and laws the LORD our God has commanded you?' tell him . . .
> (Deuteronomy 6:20–21)

The children will ask about the meaning of God's commands. They are not asking about their content, but more about their place: 'What's going on with these commands?'; 'Why should we love God and obey him?'

It would have been easy to answer just by saying, 'Because God told us to!' or 'Because it is right to do so' or 'Because he knows what's best'. All of these are true, but they are not how God tells them to reply. When asked why we should love God, they must tell their children a story:

> [T]ell him: 'We were slaves of Pharaoh in Egypt, but the LORD brought us out of Egypt with a mighty hand. Before our eyes the LORD sent signs and wonders – great and terrible – on Egypt and Pharaoh and his whole household. But he brought us out from there to bring us in and give us the land that he promised on oath to our ancestors. The LORD commanded us to obey all these decrees and to fear the LORD our God, so that we might always prosper and be kept alive, as is the case today. And if we are careful to obey all this law before the LORD our God, as he has commanded us, that will be our righteousness.'
> (Deuteronomy 6:21–25)

The answer is a summary of what God has done for his people. It's the story of salvation. We were slaves, but he rescued us. We were in Egypt but he brought us to this land. He has kept his promises. He has acted in an awesome way for our good. We have seen God at work.

The rescue from Egypt was a picture of the true salvation to come through Jesus, the ultimate Passover lamb who was sacrificed on our behalf (1 Corinthians 5:7). God has rescued us from the kingdom of darkness and brought us into the kingdom of light; he has redeemed us from slavery through Jesus (Colossians 1:12–14).

God's wonderful, gracious, saving love for us leads us to love him.

We love God because of what he's done for us, because he has set his love on us and saved us. This is why, in the New Testament, John writes, 'We love because he first loved us' (1 John 4:19). God has shown his wonderful, incredible love to us. No-one else has ever loved us, or even could love us, like this.

God's wonderful, gracious, saving love for us leads us to love him.

Loving God, and the gospel

This brings us to loving God, and the gospel. We only love God because of the gospel. There are lots of references to 'love' in the Bible, but there are far, far more about how God loves us than about how we should love him. In the next chapter of Deuteronomy, the question is raised as to why God should save his people and give them the Promised Land. The answer is simply: 'It was because the LORD loved you and kept the oath he swore' (Deuteronomy 7:8).

Throughout the Old Testament, there is reference after reference to God's 'unfailing love', his 'covenant love' or his 'abounding love'. He is the One whose love is 'as high as the heavens are above the earth' (Psalm 103:11).

In the New Testament, we're told that 'God so loved the world that he gave his one and only Son' (John 3:16). Or we read, 'God demonstrates his own love for us in this: while we were still sinners, Christ died for us' (Romans 5:8). Paul speaks about Jesus as the 'Son of God, who loved me and gave himself for me' (Galatians 2:20), and John calls out, 'See what great love the Father has lavished on us, that we should be called children of God' (1 John 3:1). It was these sorts of verses that led the great Puritan theologian John Owen to say that the greatest unkindness we could ever pay God was to doubt that he loved us.[2]

All of our talk about loving God is set against the backdrop of his loving us. We only love him because he first loved us.

That is a crucial idea to grasp. One reason why our hearts can be cold towards God is because we doubt his love for us. We might know the verses above and others like them, but we don't include ourselves in them. We think God is speaking about loving people, but we think it's referring to other people, not us. Many of us presume God is probably frowning at us right now rather than smiling at us in love. If that is how we think and feel, then our love for God won't rise very high.

So we need to tell ourselves the gospel story. God did so love me that he sent his Son for *me*. God has demonstrated his love for *me*. Jesus loved me and gave himself for *me*.

We need to go back to the gospel and drive it home to our hearts again and again. Then we shall be reassured of God's love to us and so respond to him in love.

There is a lovely story of a lady coming to love Jesus in Luke 7. Jesus is having a meal in someone's house and this woman comes in and weeps over him. She cries so much that she wets his feet with her tears, and she dries them with her hair. Then she pours perfume over his feet. Jesus says that all of this is an act of 'love' to him. He says that this woman knows her many sins have been forgiven, while the one who has been forgiven little, loves little (Luke 7:47).

Do we believe we are forgiven much? Do we love much?

We need to come back to the cross. At the cross we see our sin, our rebellion and our wickedness. And we see God's wonderful love towards us; we see his forgiveness, full and free. As we contemplate that and let it sink in, our love for God will grow.

The church leader and writer John Stott said,

> The cross is the blazing fire at which the flame of our love is kindled, but we have to get near enough to it for its sparks to fall on us.[3]

I love that image. Think of a blazing bonfire which, if you get close enough, will warm you so that you even become too hot. But if you stand at a distance, while you can still see the fire clearly, you won't feel its heat. Our love for God flows from the burning fire of the cross – but we must draw close rather than stand at a distance. We do so by being taught, being reminded, reflecting, contemplating, singing and praying about the cross. Perhaps most fully by celebrating the Lord's Supper together.

Watch your heart!

So God calls us to devoted loyalty to him; it all flows from who he is and what he's done for us. But God knows all too well that our hearts are easily drawn away from this love, and so in the rest of Deuteronomy 6 he gives us a series of warnings. The first is *not to forget God*:

> When the LORD your God brings you into the land he swore to
> your fathers, to Abraham, Isaac and Jacob, to give you – a land
> with large, flourishing cities you did not build, houses filled with
> all kinds of good things you did not provide, wells you did not
> dig, and vineyards and olive groves you did not plant – then when
> you eat and are satisfied, **be careful that you do not forget the
> LORD**, who brought you out of Egypt, out of the land of slavery.
> (Deuteronomy 6:10–12)

God pictures a time in the future when his people have arrived
at the Promised Land and are enjoying it. He knows that we
have incredibly short memories. When life is good and we're
happy, we easily forget him. We can think we have acquired
all these good things by ourselves. So God has to say, 'Be
careful! Watch your heart so that you don't forget me and stop
loving me.'

This means that the faithful Israelites needed reminders of
who God was and what he had done for them. We need the
same today. We need to tell ourselves the gospel story, and be
taught and told the gospel story, so that we don't forget.

This is particularly important when life is going well. We
need to be reminded of where we were without God and all
that he has done. The apostle Paul says, 'Remember that at that
time you were separate from Christ, excluded from citizenship
in Israel and foreigners to the covenants of the promise, without
hope and without God in the world' (Ephesians 2:12). He goes
on, 'But now in Christ Jesus you who once were far away have
been brought near by the blood of Christ' (Ephesians 2:13).

 The second warning is *not to desert God*:

> Fear the LORD your God, serve him only and take your oaths in
> his name. **Do not follow other gods**, the gods of the peoples
> around you; for the LORD your God, who is among you, is a

jealous God and his anger will burn against you, and he will destroy you from the face of the land.
(Deuteronomy 6:13–15)

God's people were going into a situation where there would be people worshipping other gods. God knows how easily we are affected by others. In the Old Testament, his people were vulnerable to being influenced by nations that worshipped Baal and other gods. And that is exactly what happened: God's people started worshipping these other gods.

We can do the same today. We can look over the fence at our neighbours or across the desk to our work colleagues and think, 'I'd like to live like them, living for comfort, or pleasure.' We can be drawn after the gods of our culture: consumerism, secularism, hedonism and more.

This starts to happen when we look more at other people with envy than at the cross with appreciation. We start to dream of how we could indulge and enjoy ourselves rather than focusing on all that God has given us. It happens when we picture God as a restrictive tyrant who is against us, rather than as our loving Father who is for us.

So Moses says, fear God and serve him alone. Don't think he's a pathetic pushover god who won't be angry with you. Stay loyal. Make him more important than anything else. Don't desert the God you should love and start following other gods instead.

We need to hear and heed that same warning today.

Lastly, we must *not test God*:

Do not put the LORD your God to the test as you did at Massah. Be sure to keep the commands of the LORD your God and the stipulations and decrees he has given you.
(Deuteronomy 6:16–17)

When Moses mentions 'Massah', he's referring to an event earlier in Israel's history (see Exodus 17:1–7). The people were in the desert and suffering from a shortage of water. Rather than trusting God and turning to him, they tested him. They doubted his goodness and thought God couldn't, or wouldn't, help them. Moses calls this 'putting God to the test'. It's an attitude that says: you need to prove yourself to me, because I don't trust you.

This temptation will come when life is hard and there are troubles of different kinds. If faced with illness or tragedy, singleness or infertility, loneliness or angst, we can turn against God and demand that he change things for us. Rather than loving him and staying loyal to him, we will be tempted to doubt and then disobey him. We start to think he owes us something or has let us down, rather than appreciating him as the God who gave his only Son for us.

We need to watch out. We can easily forget that God is the One who has given us so much and stop being grateful to him. We can desert God and run along with the gods of our age. We can test God when we find life hard, and say that he is not really with us and won't help us.

Do you believe your heart can and will do those things? If we think we're immune or that these are someone else's problem, not ours, then we really are in trouble. God warns his people here because he knows these temptations will come, and his people will have to watch themselves.

We are in the safest place when we know that it is possible to do these things. When we know how fickle our hearts can be, and we're concerned about it, then we are careful. We will pay attention to how we're thinking about God, how we're feeling towards him. We will ask ourselves whether our hearts love God or are growing cold towards him.

Not loving anything else

This call to love God above all else also means that we need to beware of loving other things. In the Bible, people are pictured as loving money, honour by others, being seen as important, themselves, or pleasure. Such loving is always presented as being in competition with God. So Jesus says we cannot love God and love money at the same time; it's like trying to serve two masters (Luke 16:13). Paul says people will be lovers of pleasure *rather* than lovers of God (2 Timothy 3:4). The point is that you cannot have two highest loyalties, only one.

This is why Jesus says we must love him more than anyone else, even our families:

> Anyone who loves their father or mother more than me is not
> worthy of me; anyone who loves their son or daughter more
> than me is not worthy of me.
> (Matthew 10:37)

We need to be clear on what Jesus is saying here. This doesn't mean we shouldn't love our family members – not at all. The key is in the comparison: 'more than me'. Remember, love is about devoted loyalty. We must not have devoted loyalty to anyone else above Jesus.

Of course, once we have devoted loyalty to Jesus and want to live for him, he will then tell us that we should love our spouse, our parents and our children. He tells us to love our neighbour as ourselves. He even tells us to love our enemies. So if we love him above all, then we will go on to love others. But our love for others flows out of our devoted loyalty to him. He is the top of the agenda, and he sets the rest of that agenda for our lives.

We need to be absolutely honest then and say that we are

tempted to love other things above Jesus. We are tempted to love money or pleasure or people.

Which is it for you? What is the rival to loving God with all your heart? What is it that could draw your heart away from God?

The need for surgery

We need to reflect on the gospel and watch our hearts, but ultimately this love for God is something God himself needs to produce in us. The sad fact is that left to ourselves, we will never love him rightly. Remember Deuteronomy? Despite all that God has done for his people, and despite his calls for them to love him, they won't. He knows they won't.

Later in the book of Deuteronomy, Moses looks ahead to the time when his people will turn away from God. Their devotion will cool and their loyalty will fade; despite his warnings, they will forget God, desert him and put him to the test. But Moses also looks ahead and speaks about what God will do as a result. One day,

> The LORD your God will circumcise your hearts and the hearts of your descendants, so that you may love him with all your heart and with all your soul, and live.
> (Deuteronomy 30:6)

Do you see what the Israelites needed? They needed God to change their hearts radically so that they would love him, and so that their love would be deep and constant. We need the same. Left to ourselves, we'll love other things. Our hearts will be hard and cold towards God. But with God's heart surgery, we will love him as we should.

That is all very humbling – we cannot do it by ourselves. It is very sobering – left to ourselves, we will never love God as we should. But it is also very encouraging – God is so committed to having people love him that he will work in us to change us. That promise is fulfilled through the work of Jesus and the Holy Spirit. God has washed us and renewed our hearts (Titus 3:5–6). If we believe in Jesus, then God has done this work in us. He has changed our hearts and turned our affections towards him so that we love him. We now ask him to make that love grow more and more.

We must still be active ourselves. We should watch our hearts, be careful not to love other things, come back to the gospel and remind ourselves of God's love for us. But we do all this knowing that we need God to work in us to bring us to love him first, and realizing that we always remain dependent on him to continue that work (Philippians 2:12–13).

So if we're not Christians, we need to ask God to change our hearts to cause us to love him in the first place. If we are those who believe in Jesus, then we shall thank him for the work he has done already. We shall ask him now to make our love grow more and more.

Picture the difference
Picture the difference between George and Andrew. They both work hard. They are both faithful and caring to their wives. They both take responsibility for their children. They are both involved in serving within their church. They both give regularly. At first glance, they look the same, but notice the difference.

George loves God. He doesn't always find living for him easy; indeed, sometimes George is tired and fed up. But he wants to live for God. A small smile plays round his lips when he thinks about God and what he has done for George. A light comes into his eyes when he thinks of Jesus dying for him. His heart is warm towards God, and he wants to live for him and please him.

Andrew's heart is growing cold. He feels duty but no warmth. He puts one foot in front of the other in the Christian life, but there's no quickness to his steps. He feels reluctant in his service, but goes through the motions more out of habit than conviction. It's not that Andrew is not necessarily a Christian (although he may not be), but in Jesus' words, he needs to return to 'the love you had at first' (Revelation 2:4), come back to the gospel and have his heart warmed with the wonder of who God is and what he has done. He needs to pray that God would fill Andrew with love for him.

Here is our first heart attitude. It doesn't get any more foundational than this. We are to be those who love God with all that we are. Love God, and do what you will.

2
fear

You will rarely hear someone called a 'God-fearing' man or woman today. If you do, the description will almost certainly be used negatively. It means someone who is scared of God, overly religious, and probably overbearing as well.

Many years ago, that phrase would have been used of someone who was considered moral and upright. It went hand in hand with being honourable and earnest. It was thought of as a good thing. But not any more.

Even in the church, we're pretty unlikely to use that description today. Just imagine you wanted to describe someone you admired as a Christian, someone who was a good example. You might say they were someone who really loved God, really lived for God or really trusted God. But you'd be unlikely to say they were someone who really feared God. If you did, people wouldn't immediately or necessarily think that was a good thing.

We've moved a very long way from the way the Bible speaks. And there's a serious gap in our thinking about 'heart attitudes', because we wouldn't include 'fear' in that list. You can tell that there's a problem, because the Bible actually speaks about fearing God far, far more frequently than it does about loving him. Admittedly, numbers don't prove everything, and loving God is foundational, as we've seen already, but the point is that this is a huge theme in the Bible that we tend to overlook.

The goodness of fear

We overlook fear because it sounds negative: fear of anything is bad. Surely, we think, God doesn't want us to be afraid of him. In fact, we might even think of all the times that God tells individuals, 'Do not fear' (and we'll come to those later). I want to whet your appetite with some verses which show us that the fear of God really is *a good thing*. Taste these and see what you think!

Probably the most famous verse on fear is this one:

> The fear of the LORD is the beginning of knowledge.
> (Proverbs 1:7)

And then later:

> The fear of the LORD is the beginning of wisdom.
> (Proverbs 9:10)

So, true knowledge and wisdom start with, and are built on, fearing God. According to the book of Proverbs, fearing God is foundational to a right life. Here are some of the later Proverbs on the subject:

> The fear of the LORD is a fountain of life,
>   turning a person from the snares of death.
> (Proverbs 14:27)

Do you see that the fear of the Lord is life-giving? It helps us avoid the snares of death. Or:

> The fear of the LORD leads to life;
>> then one rests content, untouched by trouble.
>
> (Proverbs 19:23)

The fear of the Lord brings life, rest and contentment. Already this doesn't sound like our ideas of 'fear', does it? This fear means I can relax!

In Proverbs 15, we're told:

> Better a little with the fear of the LORD
>> than great wealth with turmoil.
>
> (Proverbs 15:16)

It is much better to have the fear of God in your life and not much else than to win the lottery. No wonder we're also instructed to

> always be zealous for the fear of the LORD.
>
> (Proverbs 23:17)

Fear of God is something we should want to have. We should desire and pursue it.

In the Psalms, we're told that

> the LORD delights in those who fear him.
>
> (Psalm 147:11)

> Blessed are all who fear the LORD.
>
> (Psalm 128:1)

The LORD confides in those who fear him;
   he makes his covenant known to them.
(Psalm 25:14)

Surely his salvation is near those who fear him.
(Psalm 85:9)

Fear of God is a good thing. By contrast, not fearing God is seen as a terrible thing; it is the wicked or the foolish who have no fear of God (Psalm 36:1; Proverbs 1:7, 29). So David says,

Come, my children, listen to me;
   I will teach you the fear of the LORD.
(Psalm 34:11)

This is David inviting people to come and learn something really important.

According to God, it would be wonderful to be able to say of someone, 'He really fears God.' That's exactly what he says of Job: he boasts to Satan, 'Have you considered my servant Job? There is no one on earth like him; he is blameless and upright, a man who fears God and shuns evil' (Job 1:8). Or when Moses needs to give leadership positions to others, who does he look for? Men who fear God (Exodus 18:21). Fearing God is a good character description.

Fearing God is a good character description.

When I was first studying this aspect, I was completely struck by one verse. Now, I don't often have moments where a verse leaves me speechless and gasping, but this was one of them. It was a verse in Isaiah that describes Jesus as the Messiah who is promised to come:

The Spirit of the LORD will rest on him –
   the Spirit of wisdom and of understanding,
   the Spirit of counsel and of might,
   the Spirit of knowledge and fear of the LORD –
and he will delight in the fear of the LORD.
(Isaiah 11:2–3)

Jesus delighted in fearing God. When I first read that, I sat looking at it for a while, thinking, *you can* delight *in the fear of God? If you can delight in it, then it clearly isn't what I think it is.* Fear of God is a good thing that the Holy Spirit brings us, a good thing that we should want to have.

Right, but negative, fear

Let's think about what the fear of God actually is. To do so, we need to distinguish between two ways in which the word 'fear' is used in the Bible. First, there is a fear of God that is *right, but negative.* It is fear of God's judgment, fear of God's wrath because of sin.

We first see this type of fear back in the Garden of Eden in Genesis 3. Adam and Eve have just disobeyed God's command, and sin has entered the world. They hide from God when he comes looking for them, and Adam says they hid from him because they were *afraid* (Genesis 3:10). This is the right, but negative, fear of God because of sin. We see it throughout the Bible.

For example, Psalm 90 speaks about God's anger at people's sin and concludes,

If only we knew the power of your anger!
   Your wrath is as great as the fear that is your due.
(Psalm 90:11)

This is fear of God because of his anger and wrath. We might not feel this fear as we should; indeed, we might be oblivious to God's anger and therefore not fearful. That's why the psalmist calls out: if only we *knew* the power of your anger! But whether we feel it or not, the reality is there. Later, in the book of Hebrews, we're told that it is a 'dreadful thing' to fall into the hands of the living God (Hebrews 10:31).

The truth is that we have rebelled against God and he is the God of holy judgment. This means we should fear him. It is a fear like that of a criminal who fears the police. It is right but it is negative. This is not the fear of God that Jesus delighted in. In fact, this is the fear of God that Jesus has rescued us *from*.

There are many verses that speak about how we should not fear God's punishment because of Jesus' death in our place. The wonder of the gospel is that Jesus took God's anger and wrath so we might escape it. The result is that if we trust in Jesus, we have been rescued from this fear of God. For example, the apostle Paul writes,

> The Spirit you received does not make you slaves, so that you live in fear again; rather, the Spirit you received brought about your adoption to sonship. And by him we cry, '*Abba*, Father.'
> (Romans 8:15)

Paul says that God has given us his Spirit. But he is not a Spirit who makes us slaves so that we live in fear. God doesn't want his people tiptoeing around being afraid of him. No, he has adopted us as his children so that we can run to him in confidence. He wants us to be sure of his love and his acceptance. Similarly, John writes,

There is no fear in love. But perfect love drives out fear, because fear has to do with punishment. The one who fears is not made perfect in love.
(1 John 4:18)

The negative fear of God is because he will punish us for our sins. John's point is that God's love to us in Jesus throws that sort of fear out of the window. We can be wonderfully confident of his love.

So, if you are reading this and are not yet a Christian, then I need to say that you should indeed fear God. You face his punishment, and that is a fearful thing. But the wonderful news is that God has sent Jesus to rescue you from that punishment, so that you can be free from that fear and have real confidence in God's love and acceptance.

But if you are a Christian, please know that you have been rescued from this kind of fear. God sent Jesus so that there is no condemnation for those who believe in him (Romans 8:1); he sent his Spirit into our hearts so that we would know freedom rather than fear in our relationship with him (Romans 8:15). If you feel uncertain and hesitant in your relationship with God, then reflect on these verses and others that describe the wonderful truth of the gospel. (We'll also reflect more on this topic in the chapter on confidence later.)

So that's the first meaning of fear: the right, but negative, fear from which we're been saved.

Good, and positive, fear
Secondly, the Bible speaks much more regularly of a *good, and positive, fear* which is ongoing. This is the sort of fear we began the chapter by looking at: the fear we should want to have, and be zealous for; the fear in which we can delight. It is

difficult to give a simple definition, so let me build a composite picture for you.

Firstly, we see that this includes fear of God as the sovereign Creator:

> By the word of the LORD the heavens were made,
>   their starry host by the breath of his mouth.
> He gathers the waters of the sea into jars;
>   he puts the deep into storehouses.
> Let all the earth fear the LORD;
>   let all the people of the world revere him.
> For he spoke, and it came to be;
>   he commanded, and it stood firm.
> (Psalm 33:6–9)

There is a story about how US President Roosevelt often used to go outside with advisers and look up at the stars. After a few minutes of silent contemplation, Roosevelt would say, 'I think we feel small enough now.' That's the idea of this psalm. You look at what God has done in creation. You see that he spoke, and it was. You see the stars he made. You see that God creating the oceans is like us filling a jar with water. You let that sink in, and you stand in awe. You remember how small you are, and you are humbled. That is the call in the psalm, to let the earth *fear* and the people *revere* God.

Secondly, there is fear of God as the awesome Saviour. In the Old Testament, God rescued his people from Egypt through the Red Sea. In that same act, he defeated the Egyptians who were trying to destroy the Jews. At the end of this great act of salvation, we read this:

> And when the Israelites saw the mighty hand of the
> LORD displayed against the Egyptians, the people feared

the LORD and put their trust in him and in Moses his
servant.

(Exodus 14:31)

The people see what God has done and they stand in reverent
awe of him. But notice this is not a scared, running-away sort
of feeling. See what they do?
They fear him and *put their trust
in him.* They see how big and
mighty he is, and so they rely on
him. It's like having the greatest
big brother, whom everyone
else is afraid of because he's so
powerful, but you know he will
protect you. So, while being in awe of him, you put your hand
in his.

*So, while being
in awe of him,
you put your
hand in his.*

We see that link between fear and trust elsewhere too:

I waited patiently for the LORD;
    he turned to me and heard my cry.
He lifted me out of the slimy pit,
    out of the mud and mire;
he set my feet on a rock
    and gave me a firm place to stand.
He put a new song in my mouth,
    a hymn of praise to our God.
Many will see and fear the LORD
    and put their trust in him.

(Psalm 40:1–3)

This is David speaking about his deliverance: how God has
heard his cry and saved him, how God has given him something
to sing about. And then he says, 'Many will see and fear the

LORD.' They'll look at God's rescue of David and they'll fear God themselves. And again, they'll then 'put their trust in him'. This is a fear that means you won't run away from God, but run towards him. You're full of awe at how mighty he is, and you trust yourself to him.

Elsewhere, this fear is linked with praise and worship:

> Declare his glory among the nations,
>   his marvellous deeds among all peoples.
> For great is the LORD and most worthy of praise;
>   he is to be feared above all gods.
> (Psalm 96:3–4)

You declare God's glory – how magnificent he is. You declare what he has done – his marvellous deeds. And you say he is great, most worthy of praise, to be feared above all others. This is seeing God as bigger and better than any other god, having a picture of him that dwarfs all competitors.

This good and right fear of God does include being genuinely afraid of what God can do. Jesus addresses his disciples in Luke's Gospel:

> I tell you, my friends, do not be afraid of those who kill the body
> and after that can do no more. But I will show you whom you
> should fear: fear him who, after your body has been killed, has
> authority to throw you into hell. Yes, I tell you, fear him. Are not
> five sparrows sold for two pennies? Yet not one of them is forgotten
> by God. Indeed, the very hairs of your head are all numbered.
> Don't be afraid; you are worth more than many sparrows.
> (Luke 12:4–7)

Jesus is speaking to the disciples about what they may face as his followers: those who will kill them for being Christians.

And Jesus says that they, and we, should be more worried about what God can do than about what people can do. People can only kill your body, he says, but God can send you to hell. So be more afraid of God than people. See God as bigger, more important and more significant.

But notice this: having told them to fear God more than people, Jesus then says, 'Don't be afraid'! Literally, 'Don't fear'. Why not? Because you are valuable to God; he has the very hairs on your head numbered. So we should fear God above anyone else, but at the same time we should not fear, because he cares for us. There should be concern over God's judgment and certainty in his care: awesome reverence and confident assurance.

Here's a last reference which we would possibly never have included under 'fear':

> If you, O Lord, kept a record of sins,
>   O Lord, who could stand?
> But with you there is forgiveness;
>   therefore you are feared.
> (Psalm 130:3–4)

I should mention that this is the old NIV translation. The new NIV changes the last phrase to say: 'so that we can, with reverence, serve you'. I presume that the publishing team changed it because, at least in part, the more literal version is such a strange idea to us. If we read a verse saying, 'With you there is forgiveness, therefore . . .', we would finish it with, 'therefore you are loved', or 'thanked', or 'praised'. But here it is 'feared'.

And that is exactly what it says. It clearly can't mean being scared, because being scared doesn't come from being forgiven. This fear must have a sense of awe or reverence. It has the feel of: 'I can't believe you are so great; I stand utterly amazed at you.'

How can we sum up this fear of God?

It is not being scared of him, because it has a confidence to it, and yet it is the very opposite of taking God casually. This is one of our problems. We tend to think of confidence in someone as opposed to being in awe of them. It is as if awesome respect and confident assurance can't go together. But they can, and they do, and they must. If we focus on awesome reverence of God, we can all too easily become nervous in our relationship with him. But if we focus on confident assurance, we can easily slide into presuming on him. However, it is possible to have awesome reverence and confident assurance held together.

Imagine standing on the edge of the Grand Canyon. I am told it is an utterly awesome and overwhelming sight – it takes your breath away. Standing right on the edge and looking into it would be frightening! But there are lots of viewing platforms where you can stand behind a barrier, completely secure and safe. (I know some people would be scared even with the barrier!) But the barrier means that you are completely safe; you can lean against it; you can be confident, rather than nervous.

Now here's the point: being secure because of the barrier doesn't mean you're not overwhelmed by the sight. The barrier doesn't shrink the awesomeness. It simply means you can enjoy the view fully.

With God, we have that safety barrier: we are assured of his love and forgiveness; we are his children. Rather than being nervous, we can be confident before him, *and yet we can still be awestruck by him*. We can still 'fear him'.

Confident, awesome reverence for God

So this right and positive fear of God is a *confident, awesome reverence for God*. This is the fear of God that Jesus delighted in, the fear we can delight in ourselves. This is the fear that is the beginning of knowledge and wisdom because it means we start with a right view of God, fear that is a fountain of life because it means we are concerned with God rather than living for ourselves. It is fear that means we can rest content because we trust him. In short, this is good fear!

Think about the results of having such a fear of God. We shall:

- run to God in trouble and trust in him
- want to live for God and obey him
- hate sin and fight against it
- be faithful to God even under pressure
- be humble before God
- submit to God's will
- want to listen to God's Word to us
- long for God's glory
- be set free from the fear of people and situations

All this will be there because we have this big, magnificent, overwhelming vision of God. We know God is bigger and better than anyone or anything else. We see him as more glorious, more magnificent, more worthy.

Without this fear of God, we will easily ignore him, disobey his commands and neglect his Word. We are superficial in our relationship with him and presume on him; we are likely to be proud and full of ourselves; we are easily fearful of people and situations.

Picture two people sitting side by side at a church service. One fears God and the other doesn't. Think of the difference in how they pray: one is thoughtful and focused, the other distracted and bored. Think of the difference in how they sing: one is taken up with how great God is, and the other is thinking about whether they like the tune. Think of the difference in how they hear God's Word read and preached: one is hanging on to every word, and the other might be sending a text.

Think for a moment of the difference that fearing God makes in your daily life – for example, when a friend asks a question about your faith, and you're tempted to duck the issue, when your boss at work asks you to do something illegal or unfair, or when you're tempted into sin.

Do you see what a difference the fear of God makes?

So God says of his people,

> Oh, that their hearts would be inclined to fear me and keep all my commands always, so that it might go well with them and their children for ever!
> (Deuteronomy 5:29)

Fearing God, and the gospel

How then will we gain and grow in this fear? We have seen that the key tool in this is going to be the gospel. Other truths will come into play – for example, we can reflect on creation and see God's power, and that will help us grow in awesome reverence. We can pick particular aspects about God, like his sovereign rule or his judgment, and these will help us fear him. But reflecting on the gospel will bring the right and positive fear of God most readily.

In the gospel of Jesus, we see God most clearly. We see his justice and holiness, his hatred of sin, his power and might, his love and forgiveness, his judgment and his mercy. As we look at Jesus' death and resurrection, we see God and we grow in fear.

In fact, we can say that in becoming a Christian in the first place, we have been led, by the gospel, to fear God. We have seen something of his holiness and might, and our position before him, and we have seen something of his mercy and offer of forgiveness. In responding to the gospel, we have seen that he is bigger and more important than other people and other things. We have come to trust in him and rely on him. So, in responding to the gospel, we have come to fear God.

But that's just the beginning. As with all heart attitudes, we still need to grow in this attitude of fear. And even if we began wonderfully well, we need to preserve and cultivate it – it won't remain by itself.

So we need to return to reflect on the gospel, take the time to consider it, meditate on it and let it sink in deep enough to shape our hearts to fear. It's like going and taking a look at the Grand Canyon and having our breath taken away, again. We have to look at God in the gospel and be filled with that confident, awesome reverence once more.

We should do that individually, but also corporately when we meet as his people. We should gather together wanting to see God in the gospel more clearly, and so grow in fear of him. As we hear his Word taught, we will want to have our view of God expanded. As we sing about his majesty, power and grace, we don't want to mouth empty words, but to see again how great our God is and stand in awe of him.

We can remind, teach and encourage one another, for this is a community project. Tell each other that God is bigger and better than anyone or anything, that he is glorious. Remind each other to fear him above all else. Say to people in your church: be more worried about God than your boss; be more concerned about God than your friend.

Fear of God, and prayer

We must also pray for God's help in all this. As with loving God, we will not have this right fear by ourselves. The whole storyline of the Bible emphasizes this. God constantly calls his people in the Old Testament to fear him, and they constantly fail to do so. We can sum up the story of the Old Testament as the story of a people who should have feared God, but sadly didn't.

God says in the new covenant that he will work in us to change us. One of the promises he makes is this:

> I will give them singleness of heart and action, so that they will always fear me.
> (Jeremiah 32:39–40)

This is what God does in us through the gospel. He brings us to fear him rightly.

So, we are dependent on him. We cannot change our own hearts. We pray and ask him to do it. This is what we see King David doing in the Old Testament. He prays,

> Give me an undivided heart,
>   that I may fear your name.
> (Psalm 86:11)

The trouble is that we don't pray that sort of prayer. Why? Because we don't realize that fear of God is a good thing! We need to know that it is a great thing, that one of the best things someone could ever say of us is that we really fear God. We need to know that one of the best things someone could ever say of your church is that the people there really fear God. So pray that this will be true of you and of your church.

3
joy

Friedrich Nietzsche was the atheist who famously said, 'God is dead.' Now, I don't really read highbrow books by people like him, but I did come across a very interesting comment he made about Christians. He said, 'I would believe in their salvation if they looked a little more like people who have been saved.'

Interesting, isn't it? Christians speak about salvation, which is good news, but do we look very happy about it? Do we really look like people who have been saved? Does the good news of the gospel show in our lives?

In other words, if you are a Christian, are you joyful? Does your heart, or even your mouth, smile when you think of Jesus?

The importance of this is immense. As we saw in the introduction, if we have no joy, then the Christian life quickly becomes duty and drudgery. I remember speaking to Alison, who had come to see me about her faith. She understood the gospel very well. She could explain it to others – and indeed did so. She took part in Bible studies and sang in the music group on Sundays. But she said, 'I'm doing the right things and know they are good, but I have no joy in any of it.' The result was that she constantly felt like she was going through the motions as a Christian.

Of course, we should still do the right thing no matter what our heart is feeling. But as we saw at the start of this book, without key heart attitudes, our faith can become external and, at worst, hypocritical. That is particularly true of joy.

Looking for joy

It has been well documented that our society today, despite being better off overall than previous generations, is less happy. People have come to realize that having a good standard of living doesn't necessarily bring you joy. As a result, our society is often looking for something that will bring a smile to their face. You can buy books to help you, such as *The Joy of Living*, written, we're told, by 'the happiest man in the world'. It's alive and well in advertising too: Cadbury's sell chocolate under the tagline: 'Share the joy.'

Most of us know that a self-help book is unlikely to transform our lives (although we sometimes wonder). And we know that buying chocolate won't really make us feel happier (although we still buy it). But these are surely symptoms of a deeper issue: we are a society that is wondering where real happiness lies. That desire is often what drives us in our relationships, careers, hobbies, and more. We do a lot of what we do because we think we'll feel happier as a result. We are searching for joy.

If you're not a Christian, I want to tell you that joy is ultimately found only in the Christian message. If you are a Christian, I want to urge you to grasp that truth more firmly and believe it more deeply.

The danger is that while Christians have a great source of joy in Jesus, it can remain untapped. We're sitting on a goldmine, but we don't realize it.

And that means we'll be tempted to look for joy elsewhere – despite our riches, we trade in Monopoly money! The ultimate danger is that Christians, ignoring the joy of salvation, will look no different from their non-Christian neighbour in the world of joy. We will rejoice and mourn over the same things. We will pursue joy through the same means. We need to discover the heart attitude of joy that we can have as those who trust in Christ.

Despite our riches, we trade in Monopoly money!

Joy flowing from salvation

The book of Acts tells us about the spread of the good news of salvation in Jesus. It expanded in ever-widening circles from Jerusalem. As it did so, and people came to believe in Jesus, it left joy in its wake.

We read this about the first group of believers in Jerusalem:

> They broke bread in their homes and ate together with glad and sincere hearts, praising God.
>
> (Acts 2:46–47)

Their hearts were 'glad'. In fact, the word Luke uses means 'great joy'. And we see that this flowed out into praise of God.

Later in Acts, the message spread into Samaria through Philip. He tells people about Jesus, and Luke concludes,

> So there was great joy in that city.
>
> (Acts 8:8)

We read the same thing of specific individuals. In the city of Philippi, a jailer comes to faith through Jesus:

> The jailer brought them into his house and set a meal before them; he was filled with joy because he had come to believe in God – he and his whole household.
> (Acts 16:34)

The jailer has come to believe in God and his promises of salvation through Jesus, and the result is that he is filled with joy.

Can you see how the spread of the gospel results in the spread of joy?

What is described in the book of Acts is then explained more fully in some of the New Testament letters. Peter writes to believers whose lives were hard in many ways, and yet he says,

> Though you have not seen him, you love him; and even though you do not see him now, you believe in him and are filled with an inexpressible and glorious joy, for you are receiving the end result of your faith, the salvation of your souls.
> (1 Peter 1:8–9)

The believers are filled with joy because they know they are being saved. And no wonder! The message about Jesus is good news. It tells us that our rebellion against God can be forgiven. God will wipe away our sin and guilt. We can receive his Holy Spirit and be made new. We become his children and can call him Father. We have a great future hope.

Plus, all these wonderful truths come to us through God's grace, undeserved but freely given. What we actually deserved was wrathful condemnation, but what we have received is wonderful acceptance. When we understand the gospel and see what God has done – when we know salvation, forgiveness, adoption and new life by his gracious gift – then we will feel happy about it.

If you are a Christian, then I expect you will know this already. There will have been times when you have seen your sin against God clearly, and you have seen his forgiveness, and you have seen that Jesus died in your place. You've seen how wonderful the gospel is, and you've smiled as a result.

Working for joy

But it's not as simple as that, is it?

All that I've said above is completely true. Yet we don't automatically feel joyful all the time. Yes, there are times when joy simply rises up in our hearts because of the gospel, but there are other times when that joy seems very far away indeed.

I remember eating breakfast with Pete, and he stared down at his sausage and eggs as he spoke. He was explaining how hard life was, the pressure he was under and how down he felt. In a tone of great sadness, he said, 'Within all this, I feel nothing towards God.'

You may know that sort of experience yourself, and it raises a number of questions. For example, how should we feel about sad events in our life? Does this focus on joy leave no room for tears? We'll return to that question soon. For now though, focus on this thought: while the gospel is good news, this doesn't mean that joy will always flow by itself automatically.

This is clear in Paul's ministry. He said to the Philippians that he was working for their 'progress and joy in the faith' (Philippians 1:25). His ministry to them was so that they would make progress in the faith and grow in joy in the faith. That is key for two reasons. Firstly, it means that Paul thought that 'joy in the faith' was important; it was what he wanted to see in the churches he planted. But secondly, it means that he knew it would not be automatic. He needed to work and minister to people to bring such joy. It might be there by itself as people came to believe the gospel, but it would also be a lifelong pursuit.

This is why, later in his letter to the same church, Paul commands joy:

> Rejoice in the Lord always. I will say it again: rejoice!
> (Philippians 4:4)

Here is a command to have joy in God. We tend to think that our joy or happiness is uncontrollable. That's part of how our culture thinks about emotion generally: our feelings just happen; we can't actually command them. In some ways, that's perfectly true – I can't just tell myself to be joyful and immediately feel happiness in my heart. But that doesn't mean we have no control or influence over our joy, as otherwise Paul's words don't make any sense.

There's a really crucial example of this in Luke 10. Jesus has just sent his disciples out on a preaching tour. This is how they come back:

> The seventy-two returned with joy and said, 'Lord, even the
> demons submit to us in your name.'
> (Luke 10:17)

They are rejoicing over their new-found abilities. Jesus first agrees with them:

> He replied, 'I saw Satan fall like lightning from heaven. I
> have given you authority to trample on snakes and scorpions

and to overcome all the power of the enemy; nothing will
harm you.'
(Luke 10:18–19)

Jesus basically says, 'I know you've struck a blow against Satan
– that's because I gave you that authority.' But he wants to
redirect their joy. He goes on:

> 'However, do not rejoice that the spirits submit to you, but rejoice
> that your names are written in heaven.'
> (Luke 10:20)

So, while Jesus agrees that his disciples have done some great
things in casting out demons, he tells them not to rejoice in
that, but to rejoice that their names are written in heaven.
He's saying, 'Rejoice in your salvation rather than in your
abilities.'

Jesus must mean that we can *choose* what to rejoice in. He
says, don't rejoice in *that* but in *this*. How does that work?
He is telling them: value your salvation more than your
abilities; see your salvation as more important, more precious,
and so rejoice in it.

I think of my kids when they're opening presents. As
the wrapping paper comes off, you see their face: sometimes it's a smile, grinning like mad; sometimes it's sadness
and disappointment (adults can feel the same, but we are
better at hiding it). Why do they react differently? It
all depends on what they think of the present, and how
valuable it is to them. The greater its value, the greater
their joy.

So, Jesus is telling his disciples to value their salvation above
everything else – even above good things like the authority
they've been given.

Tim Keller speaks about our rejoicing like this:

> To rejoice is to treasure a thing, to assess its value to you, to reflect on its beauty and importance until your heart rests in it and tastes the sweetness of it.[1]

Here's the point: we have choices over what we value, what we prize. So we can *choose* to rejoice in God's salvation. We can reflect on its beauty and importance. This must be something we can choose to do, otherwise it couldn't be a command. The other side of the coin is that if we are not joyful in our salvation, this tells us that we're not valuing our salvation as we should. Jesus' command then is to change our values, change our assessment, so that we rejoice rightly.

In practice, then, the key to joy in the Christian life is not simply telling ourselves to be more joyful, but to *value God's gift of salvation*.

Joy and the gospel

So the gospel brings joy, but we need to work at that joy. It involves a deliberate valuing of the gospel. But what will that mean in practice?

Firstly, we need to be taught the gospel. The better we understand it, the greater our appreciation will be. We should never think we've understood the gospel, so now we can move on to more interesting topics. As parents, my wife and I have read the Bible to our kids for many years now, and they've also studied it at church. This has meant that they're pretty familiar with the popular stories. One of our sons went through a phase a while ago when he would regularly ask, 'Can't we do something new?' His point was that he was very familiar with what he was being told, and so there was no need to do it again.

But that can never be true of the story of the gospel (and so, of course, never really true of any story in the Bible!). We should aim to drill down deeper into the truths of the gospel, to comprehend it more, and therefore value it and rejoice in it. Deeper understanding should lead to greater joy.

Secondly, we need to be reminded of the gospel. Even if I don't learn anything new, I still need to hear the good news of Jesus' life, death and resurrection, and all that he achieved. I need to be reminded of it because, although I may know it, I don't always appreciate it. I need the gospel put in front of me, to be shown off to me, so that I'm reminded of how great it is and consequently rejoice in it.

Deeper understanding should lead to greater joy.

Imagine owning a precious diamond. You keep it in a drawer and never look at it. You know it's yours and picture it in your mind, and think of it as a good thing to own. But compare that to taking it out and holding it up to the light, perhaps placing it on display and getting an expert to talk you through its features. I bet your feelings about it would soon change as a result!

We need not just to know about the gospel, but also to look at it and have it presented to us again so that we truly appreciate it.

We can do this for ourselves by reminding ourselves of it. I often use key verses written out on a card, taking one verse at a time which tells me about the great truth of the gospel and spending a few minutes reading it over, reminding myself of it and pondering it. Here are three of my favourites:

For as high as the heavens are above the earth,
  so great is his love for those who fear him;

as far as the east is from the west,
> so far has he removed our transgressions from us.

(Psalm 103:11–12)

For he has rescued us from the dominion of darkness and brought us into the kingdom of the Son he loves, in whom we have redemption, the forgiveness of sins.

(Colossians 1:13–14)

'Come now, let us settle the matter,'
> says the LORD.

'Though your sins are like scarlet,
> they shall be as white as snow;

though they are red as crimson,
> they shall be like wool.

(Isaiah 1:18)

I'm not necessarily expecting to learn anything new, but I am expecting to walk away valuing the gospel more.

We can also do this for one another too. We can speak of the greatness of the gospel, the wonder of God's grace and the glory of forgiveness. We can do this in more formal times when we gather as a church; we can do it informally as we chat together. Here's a challenge for us: does the way we speak to one another show that we value our salvation above all else? If it doesn't, then we're not helping one another in our pursuit of joy.

Thirdly, we should express our joy in song. This is something we see in the Psalms. Many psalms speak of joy in salvation, and that joy is then expressed in song. For example:

My lips will shout for joy
> when I sing praise to you –

I whom you have delivered.
(Psalm 71:23)

Sing for joy to God our strength;
    shout aloud to the God of Jacob!
(Psalm 81:1)

Our mouths were filled with laughter,
    our tongues with songs of joy.
Then it was said among the nations,
    'The Lord has done great things for them.'
The Lord has done great things for us,
    and we are filled with joy.
(Psalm 126:2–3)

These psalms all involve people seeing God's goodness to them, seeing something of his salvation and responding with joy. Music allows us to express our joy more easily. When we are 'filled with joy' over our salvation, then singing songs of joy flows easily. At other times, we won't feel like singing, and yet we're told to express our joy in song anyway. For example, in Psalm 13, David is expressing his sorrow and calling out to God for help in his trouble. Yet he finishes the psalm like this:

But I trust in your unfailing love;
    my heart rejoices in your salvation.
I will sing the Lord's praise,
    for he has been good to me.
(Psalm 13:5–6)

We can call ourselves to rejoice in God even at times when, like David, we really don't feel like doing it. Often our experience will be that expressing joy in song will help us to know and feel such joy. But even if it doesn't, it is still the right thing to do.

Lastly, we should pray for this joy. That was what Paul did as he worked for people's progress and joy in the faith. For example, he prays for the Christians in Rome:

> May the God of hope fill you with all joy and peace as you trust in him.
>
> (Romans 15:13)

And his prayer in Colossians 1 includes

> . . . giving joyful thanks to the Father, who has qualified you to share in the inheritance of his holy people in the kingdom of light.
>
> (Colossians 1:12)

Paul prays regularly that people will grow in joy. As in all areas of the Christian life, while we work hard and give ourselves to something, it is ultimately God's work in us, and so we pray for it.

Joy beyond the gospel

The primary source of joy in the Bible is God's goodness to us in salvation, but joy should be expressed over more things than the gospel. We value what is connected to it and what it teaches us to value.

Here are some examples:

- Paul rejoiced that the gospel was being spread, even from bad motives (Philippians 1:18).
- James tells us to rejoice in trials, because they bring maturity which is more valuable than our comfort (James 1:2–3).

- John tells us he has great joy to know that other people are walking in the faith (2 John 4).
- Paul rejoices that the church in Corinth is concerned for him (2 Corinthians 7:7).
- Paul says he will be filled with joy at seeing Timothy again (2 Timothy 1:4).

We should rejoice over all we know that is good and right. So we rejoice in people coming to faith, Christian growth and ongoing discipleship. We rejoice to see generosity or forgiveness or sacrifice. We rejoice in good relationships, in love and care, and in material provision. God gives us many good things in life – food, friends and fun – all of which are right to rejoice in. In other words, rejoicing in the gospel doesn't mean that we should remain unmoved in the rest of life.

Speaking personally, I rejoice in my lovely and loving wife, my great kids, good friends, a fantastic church and so much more. I don't rejoice in them more than salvation, but salvation certainly doesn't relegate these things to being worthless. In fact, the gospel teaches me the importance of such people and things.

But this has a flip side. We need to *beware of overvaluing unimportant things*. We must recognize that what we value, and thus take joy in, is too easily dictated by our culture. We could rejoice in a new car, a better job, a house extension or our football team's success. Some of those things will be perfectly good things. It is not that we don't value them at all, but we must not overvalue them. Consider these proverbs:

> Better a dish of vegetables with love
>   than a fattened calf with hatred.
> (Proverbs 15:17)

Better a dry crust with peace and quiet
> than a house full of feasting, with strife.

(Proverbs 17:1)

The gospel teaches me that relationships are more important than the size of my TV. Kindness and forgiveness in a family are more valuable than an expensive holiday. If we're not careful here, then our joy will be no different from that of our non-Christian neighbours.

Joys and sorrows

Valuing the rest of life rightly leads us to the question of sorrow. Consider this quote from Edward T. Welch:

> It is a myth that faith is always smiling. The truth is that faith often feels like the very ordinary process of dragging one foot in front of the other because we are conscious of God.[2]

Does this undermine all we've been saying about joy? Not at all! All this talk of joy doesn't mean that Christians walk around with inane grins on their faces. Rather, Christians should know ongoing joy in salvation, but they will feel great sadness and sorrow as well.

Christians are those who know how the world is supposed to be. So, when we see the world marred by sin, and see people causing hurt and pain, we are obviously sad. When we see lives wrecked by illness, separated by death or struck with tragedy, we may cry. In fact, we could argue that Christians have reason to be more sorrowful than non-Christians, because we know how wrong such things are. We know that this is not how God made the world.

So, in the Psalms, we see cries of despair as well as joy (see Psalm 13). In the Gospels, we see Jesus weeping at Lazarus' tomb because of the wrongness of death (John 11:33–35). We see Paul in anguish over other Christians because he fears they are not trusting the gospel (Galatians 4:19–20). Paul, the man who tells us to 'rejoice always', also says he has unceasing anguish in his heart because of people rejecting the gospel (Romans 9:2). These verses don't paint a picture of constant smiles.

Remember, Paul tells us not only to rejoice with those who rejoice, but also to mourn with those who mourn (Romans 12:15). We must then have an expectation of sadness as well as of joy. Beware of the always-happy, smiling Christian.

And yet we still read of joy within grief, and gladness within sorrow. Peter writes to suffering Christians,

> In all this you greatly rejoice, though now for a little while you may have had to suffer grief in all kinds of trials.
> (1 Peter 1:6)

He has been speaking of the wonder of salvation and our future hope. In this we rejoice. But in our 'trials', we suffer grief.

Do you see the picture being painted? If we value rightly and our priorities are in line with God's, then we will respond with joy and sorrow in all the events of life. We will cry over what is sad and wrong, and rejoice over what is good and right. But even within all that variation, there should be an *underlying joy in God*. Even in the hardest of times, where we may rightly weep, the heart attitude of joy can still be present.

Horatio Spafford was a hymn writer in the nineteenth century. His wife and four daughters were travelling from the United States to England when, tragically, their ship was in a collision. His wife survived but their four daughters were all drowned. I have three children whom I love greatly, and I find it hard to comprehend such a tragedy happening to me. I know that I would be devastated.

Horatio himself was later travelling on a ship making the same journey across the Atlantic. On that journey he wrote a hymn. The first verse goes like this:

When peace like a river attends all my way,
when sorrows like sea billows roll,
whatever my lot you have taught me to say,
it is well, it is well with my soul.

Horatio Spafford knew that there would be times when life was full of peace, but there would also be times when 'sorrows like sea billows roll'. We will rightly have mixed emotions: peace and joy, sorrow and sadness. But within it, we can still say, 'It is well with my soul.' The hymn goes on to speak about God's goodness in salvation, sin being removed by Christ, and our future hope. And so, whatever sadness there is, we can still say, 'It is well with my soul.' We can still rejoice in God.

A life of joy

Do you know someone who is full of joy in God? Someone who so values God's goodness in salvation that it brings them ongoing gladness?

If you do, then I expect you'll see other things in their life as well. You'll find them living for God and serving him, and doing so gladly. You'll find that they are generous people, because joy over what we have been given means we shall love to give (see 2 Corinthians 8:2–3). You'll find that these people accept sacrifice without grumbling or complaining (see Hebrews 10:34). You'll find that they resist temptation and fight against sin because they know that God is good.

The great Bible commentator Matthew Henry wrote these words:

> The joy of the Lord will arm us against the assaults of our spiritual enemies and put our mouths out of taste for those pleasures with which the tempter baits his hooks.[3]

Joy in God means our spiritual taste buds have changed. We value God. We value his grace and gifts.

People who rejoice in God keep going even when life is hard. The American author, speaker and painter Joni Eareckson Tada was confined to a wheelchair as a teenager after a diving accident. She has been an inspiration to many in how to trust God within hardship. She wrote these words:

Joy in God means our spiritual taste buds have changed.

> You don't have to be alone in your hurt! Comfort is yours. Joy is an option. And it's all been made possible by your Saviour. He went without comfort so you might have it. He postponed joy so you might share in it. He willingly chose isolation so you might never be alone in your hurt and sorrow.[4]

I think of Maurice. He's an elderly man and his health isn't great now. There have been a variety of family tragedies – some more common, some rare and desperate. But Maurice is a man of joy. He is usually smiling. When he prays, he is full of thanksgiving and praise for all that God has done for him.

I want to be more like Maurice. I want to grow in joy. I want to cry over the pains and suffering of life, but still rejoice in the Lord. I want to pray that God would fill me with joy as I trust in him. And I want to do so until the day when our salvation is complete and we will rejoice around God's throne, and nothing will interrupt that joy. Ever.

4
peace

Everyone is anxious. At least a bit. At least sometimes.

There is a spectrum of anxiety, and we are all at different places on this. I think of Mike, who seems unruffled and unbothered even when disaster is looming. You'd describe him as 'laid back'. But even he admits to moments of lying awake at night with thoughts buzzing round his head. Then I think of Claudia, who seems to get worried about what to have for breakfast. You'd describe her as 'twitchy'. She readily admits to being a worrier.

Where are you on the spectrum?

All sorts of things will play into our experience of anxiety: our background and upbringing, our personality and character, our situation and relationships. There is huge variation between us – and we should understand and respect that. Respect is important, as otherwise it's very easy for people like Claudia to feel condemned, and for people like Mike to feel smug.

We must realize that our battles with anxiety are not the

same as other people's. If someone else struggles with anxiety more or less than you do, that doesn't immediately mean they are more or less godly or trusting than you. How do you know, for example, the way you'd react if you had their background and lived in their situation?

Plus, we all wrestle with anxiety at some level. We are all engaged in the same fight, even if the battle lines are drawn in different places for different people. So let's acknowledge that up front, and let's each look to grow in our experience of God's peace.

The wonderful news is that God's people can be character-ized by a trust that means that they know peace rather than worry, calm rather than fretting. And God doesn't want to condemn us for our anxieties. He may challenge us as to whether we are trusting him, but the main thing he wants to do is reassure us.

The most common command

Do you know what is the most common command in the whole Bible? It's not about worshipping God or loving God, nor about obedience.

It is: 'Do not fear.' It comes from God's mouth many, many times. Here's a sampling:

> After this, the word of the LORD came to Abram in a vision:
> 'Do not be afraid, Abram.
>> I am your shield,
>> your very great reward.'
> (Genesis 15:1)

> That night the LORD appeared to him and said, 'I am the God of your father Abraham. Do not be afraid, for I am with you.'
> (Genesis 26:24)

The Lord said to Moses, 'Do not be afraid of him, for I have delivered him into your hands, along with his whole army and his land.'
(Numbers 21:34)

But the Lord said to him, 'Peace! Do not be afraid. You are not going to die.'
(Judges 6:23)

He said: 'Listen, King Jehoshaphat and all who live in Judah and Jerusalem! This is what the Lord says to you: "Do not be afraid or discouraged because of this vast army. For the battle is not yours, but God's."'
(2 Chronicles 20:15)

'Do not be afraid, you worm Jacob,
    little Israel, do not fear,
for I myself will help you,' declares the Lord,
    your Redeemer, the Holy One of Israel.
(Isaiah 41:14)

This is what the Lord says –
    he who made you, who formed you in the womb,
    and who will help you:
Do not be afraid, Jacob, my servant,
    Jeshurun, whom I have chosen.
(Isaiah 44:2)

'Do not be afraid of them, for I am with you and will rescue you,' declares the Lord.
(Jeremiah 1:8)

Do not be afraid of the king of Babylon, whom you now fear. Do not be afraid of him, declares the Lord,

for I am with you and will save you and deliver you from
his hands.
(Jeremiah 42:11)

Do not lose heart or be afraid
    when rumours are heard in the land;
one rumour comes this year, another the next,
    rumours of violence in the land
    and of ruler against ruler.
(Jeremiah 51:46)

One night the Lord spoke to Paul in a vision: 'Do not be afraid;
keep on speaking, do not be silent.'
(Acts 18:9)

Many of these commands not to fear are given to particular
people in particular situations. But do you see how God is
concerned generally about the fears and worries of his people?
He is alert to the fact that we are worried, and he wants to
address that worry, to reassure us.

Hear some of Jesus' words:

Therefore I tell you, do not worry about your life, what you will
eat or drink; or about your body, what you will wear. Is not life
more than food, and the body more than clothes?
(Matthew 6:25)

Jesus goes on to speak about not worrying four more times
in this passage. We'll look at what he says in more detail below,
but for now, just get hold of the idea that Jesus is worried
about our tendency to worry!

I used to think of these sorts of verses as challenging ones.
They said to me, 'You *should not* worry!' So I'd use the verses to

tell myself not to. And that can be right. But first we should see these verses as reassuring ones. They say, 'You *need not* worry.'

What type of peace are we aiming for?

We need to clarify some issues here. What is it that we're aiming at with this heart attitude? Are we expecting to be people who are constantly serene and peaceful? Are we expecting to float through life untroubled by any situation or challenge?

That's not what we see in Jesus. The most emotional we see him is in the Garden of Gethsemane. We're told:

> He took Peter, James and John along with him, and he began to be deeply distressed and troubled. 'My soul is overwhelmed with sorrow to the point of death,' he said to them. 'Stay here and keep watch.'
>
> (Mark 14:33–34)

That's not a picture of someone remaining 'serene'. Of course, it was perfectly appropriate for Jesus to express such distress, because he was facing the prospect of the cross the next day. The point is simply that trusting God does not mean feeling 'calm' in every situation.

The apostle Paul says in his letter to the Philippians, 'Do not be anxious about anything', and reassures us that 'the peace of God, which transcends all understanding, will guard your hearts and your minds in Christ Jesus' (Philippians 4:6–7). So here is a man who thought our hearts should be at peace. We might start painting that idealized picture of a 'calm', 'serene' Christian once again.

But earlier in the same letter, Paul talks about his companion Epaphroditus. He had been seriously ill but had recovered. Paul is sending him back home to Philippi and says this:

> Therefore I am all the more eager to send him, so that when you see him again you may be glad and I may have less anxiety.
> (Philippians 2:28)

Paul says he will sleep easier at night knowing that Epaphroditus is back at home. We could respond: 'But Paul, why didn't you just follow your own command not to be anxious about anything and to know God's peace?'

Elsewhere, Paul says, 'I face daily the pressure of my concern for all the churches' (2 Corinthians 11:28). He uses the same word as in Philippians: this is his *anxiety* for the churches. Again, we could ask, 'Paul, why don't you just pray and trust God?'

However, Paul doesn't have one rule for himself and another for the rest of us. There is such a thing as *appropriate concern*, or even *reasonable worry*. If I received news that one of my children had been hit by a car and was in intensive care, I would not be supposed to stay relaxed. If my church was in trouble and faced an uncertain future, I would not be supposed to remain unmoved. We are not aiming at a tranquil life where we don't react to worrying situations.

But there is also such a thing as *inappropriate anxiety*, or *sinful worry*. That is what Jesus and Paul command against. That is what we too want to fight.

Knowing the borderline between these two is tricky. And of course, even within the areas of reasonable concern, my trust in God should make a difference. I know that my child in hospital is still under his sovereign rule. So within my right concerns I can trust him for the future. But we must still distinguish between these two, as otherwise we'll be aiming at the wrong thing.

So here's our aim: we want to fight against sinful worry where we are not trusting God; we want to grow in knowing a heart attitude of peace.

Do not worry about what?

So let's look at what Jesus says about worry. We saw his opening words above, and they are worth repeating:

> Therefore I tell you, do not worry about your life, what
> you will eat or drink; or about your body, what you will
> wear. Is not life more than food, and the body more than
> clothes?
> (Matthew 6:25)

Jesus focuses in on two particular aspects of worry: food and clothing. This is worry of the most basic kind: how we will live. We want to be sure that we will have enough food on the table and clothes on our backs. We could extend this to being able to pay the bills and the rent or a mortgage. Inevitably, it is all wrapped up in the issue of money.

Unsurprisingly, Jesus has just been speaking about serving God and money. His point was that you cannot do both. Rather, he describes his followers as those who serve God alone and store up treasure in heaven rather than on earth (Matthew 6:19–24). That's the background for Jesus' opening word: 'Therefore'.

Putting it in context like that helps us to see how reassuring Jesus' words are. He's just been saying, 'Don't store up money here; serve God, not money!' Our inevitable response is: 'But what about paying the bills? What about saving for my old age?' So Jesus immediately reassures us, 'Therefore, do not worry about your life . . .'

He then breaks down his argument, beginning with the issue of food:

> Look at the birds of the air; they do not sow or reap or store away
> in barns, and yet your heavenly Father feeds them. Are you not

much more valuable than they? Can any one of you by worrying
add a single hour to your life?
(Matthew 6:26–27)

The birds don't store up food, and yet God feeds them. Here's
a picture of God's sovereign provision for his creation. Listen
to Jesus' words of reassurance: are you not *much more valuable*
than birds! If God bothers to provide for our feathered friends,
then will he not also provide for us? If a parent remembers to
feed their dog, don't you think they'll also feed their children?

There's an immediate, reassuring challenge to us: do we
believe we are valuable to God? Do we believe he cares? It's a
reassuring challenge because answering it positively should
lead us towards peace. It's a reassuring *challenge* because we
can all too easily answer it negatively. So hear Jesus trying to
persuade you: God feeds the birds; he'll feed you. Are you not
much more valuable to him?

Then Jesus moves to clothing:

And why do you worry about clothes? See how the flowers of the
field grow. They do not labour or spin. Yet I tell you that not even
Solomon in all his splendour was dressed like one of these. If that
is how God clothes the grass of the field, which is here today and
tomorrow is thrown into the fire, will he not much more clothe
you – you of little faith?
(Matthew 6:28–30)

The argument runs in a similar way. The flowers in the field
do not work and yet end up beautifully clothed, more beautiful
than Solomon in his best outfit. If that's what God does
with fields, don't you think he'll clothe you? After all, grass is
insignificant; it can be here today and gone tomorrow. But
you are significant to God.

Again, the simple reassuring challenge is: do we believe that? Jesus calls his disciples those of 'little faith' because they are struggling to believe this, to trust that God cares and so will provide.

Jesus sums it up and issues his command again:

> So do not worry, saying, 'What shall we eat?' or 'What shall we drink?' or 'What shall we wear?' For the pagans run after all these things, and your heavenly Father knows that you need them.
> (Matthew 6:31–32)

'Don't worry about the material stuff of life,' Jesus says. The pagans, people who don't know God, run after such things. They spend their life pursuing these things, and so worrying about them. But Christians are to be different because they have a heavenly Father who knows what they need.

I was studying this passage with a friend on the day I started writing this chapter. He had recently become a father. So I made the point referring to his son: 'Wouldn't you make sure Peter had enough to eat and wear? You wouldn't dream of not taking care of him, would you? You know what he needs and how precious he is to you.' Similarly, God is our heavenly Father who knows what we need. If that is our vision of God, our hearts can be at peace.

This means that peace is not found in reorganizing our work–life balance, or in breathing techniques, or in medication (even if there is a place for some of these sometimes). It is found in knowing God.

Peace and changing what we live for

Within Jesus' reassuring words, however, there is a deeper challenge. We noticed it above in passing. Jesus had challenged his disciples to 'store up treasure in heaven' rather than on earth. He had told them they could not serve two masters, God and money. In other words, he was saying what his followers would live for, what they thought the purpose of life was. That led him into his reassurance that God would take care of them.

Jesus returns to the bigger perspective:

> But seek first his kingdom and his righteousness, and all these things will be given to you as well.
> (Matthew 6:33)

Remember that Jesus said that the pagans 'run' after what they will eat, drink and wear. Now he uses the same word for his followers, but they are to run after, or 'seek', God's kingdom and righteousness. When they do, God will make sure they have the physical provision they need as well.

So here's a second command from Jesus. As well as the prohibition, do not worry, there is the positive command to seek first God's kingdom and righteousness. Live for God, not things. Store up treasure in heaven, not earth. This positive command is Jesus' main topic; the reassurance not to worry finds its place within it.

Live for God, not things.

So what does it mean to seek God's kingdom and righteousness?

The kingdom refers to God's rule. The big picture of the Bible is that God is bringing his rule through Jesus. That's why some of Jesus' first words are: 'Repent, for the kingdom of heaven has come near' (Matthew 4:17). The world currently lives in rebellion against God and under his judgment, but we can now enter his kingdom, come under his rule and be his subjects.

This is the spiritual reality of the world. It is not less real than the physical realities we see around us. In fact it is more real, but unseen. The kingdom of darkness is gradually receding, and God's kingdom is advancing. Jesus is calling us to get in line with what God is doing. To seek his kingdom is to enter into, and live out, life in the kingdom.

God's righteousness is similar. It means to live life in line with God's standards, in submission to his will. Jesus has already spoken about hungering and thirsting for righteousness (Matthew 5:6), living for him in a way which might even result in being persecuted (5:10). He has spoken about our acts of righteousness in living for God, which God will reward (6:1).

So, Jesus doesn't just say, 'Stop worrying.' That will never work. He tells us to replace our concern with material provision with a greater spiritual concern. Knowing God's peace only comes as part of that bigger reorientation of our hearts.

We so easily live for the here and now. Life is about what we have, what we eat and wear. In other words, it's about treasure here. If that's how we view the world, then our hearts will be wrapped up in the present, and we will worry about such things. We seek what we think is most important, and we worry about what we seek. That is often food and clothing, money and possessions. Or it might be image and achievement, career and relationships. But whatever we are living for, that is what we will seek and worry over. Our worries always reveal our deepest values. As Jesus says, 'Where your treasure is, there your heart will be also' (Matthew 6:21).

Jesus is calling us to view life differently, to see life as being about God and his kingdom.

Do you see that Jesus is not simply giving us the reassurance that God cares and will provide? If he did that, then we could go on unchanged, thinking life was all about food and clothing. We could go on storing up treasure on earth. Only now, we're reassured that God will help us with our stockpiling. Jesus' plan is much bigger: he wants to reorient our hearts and lives, wants us to see what is most important. Only when we do that will our hearts be at peace.

So let's think of some examples. We can easily be worried about work pressure and demands. We can be concerned over our career, whether we'll get promoted, for example, or we can be worried about losing our job or getting paid enough. Jesus wants to reassure us about such things, but he also wants to reorientate our hearts. Life is not ultimately about our career path. Jesus wants us to seek God's kingdom and righteousness in our work, not our security and success. He wants us to change what a 'successful' career will look like. As we make that change, we can know his peace.

Or consider children. Parents worry over their children's education, their friendships, whether or not they'll get on in life, do well, find a spouse, and much more. Again, Jesus wants to reassure us, but he also wants to reorientate us. He wants us to look at our children with the priorities of his kingdom and righteousness. That doesn't just mean that our children come to faith – it shapes what we think a 'good' life will look like for them. So now, difficulties in friendships might be an opportunity for them to grow, not simply a problem to be solved.

You see, it is possible to know God but still live for the same things as our non-Christian neighbours and colleagues, with the same agenda and priorities. The result is that we end up with the same worries. Jesus calls us to something much bigger and better, where we live for God and follow his agenda. It is within that change that we will find peace.

Peace and the gospel

All of this leads us to peace and the gospel. As with each heart attitude, we're considering the gospel as the dynamic that will produce and sustain it, and we've already seen some of that in action above. It is the gospel message about God's kingdom that lies behind our having peace.

The gospel teaches us what is most important in life: there are spiritual realities now and a physical future to come. These all shout at us: life is not about how big your TV is or what holidays you go on!

Jesus tells a parable to emphasize this point. It's the parable of the 'rich fool' (Luke 12:13–21), a farmer who is doing well in his business, so he plans to build bigger barns, store up his produce and sit back and relax. He says to himself, 'Take life easy; eat, drink and be merry.' But Jesus says that that very night the farmer will die. His great provision will be of no use to him then.

Jesus' point is that

> . . . life does not consist in an abundance of possessions.
> (Luke 12:15)

That's the first thing the gospel teaches us. Instead, life is about relationship with God, being in his kingdom. If that's our view, then we will seek God's kingdom, be more concerned about him than about what we have. This fundamental change of perspective is foundational to being at peace.

One of our big problems then is that we can believe the gospel but not believe the worldview it teaches us. We trust God for forgiveness, but we still think life is about treasure on earth. We rejoice at being adopted into God's family, but we still run after what we will eat and drink.

Do you see now how significant our worries can be? They

can show how deeply we believe the gospel. Counsellor Ed
Welch says,

> Worry, therefore, is not simply an emotion that erodes our
> quality of life or a pain to be alleviated. It is a misdirected
> love that should be confessed. It is trying to manage our world
> apart from God. It is making life about our needs, desires,
> and wants.[1]

Spend some time reflecting on these questions:

- What do I live for?
- What do I think is most important?
- Jesus said, 'Life does not consist in an abundance of
  possessions.' What do I think life consists in?
- What do my anxieties reveal about what I value most?

The second thing the gospel teaches us is that God cares. God
is so concerned about us he goes to extraordinary lengths
to save us. The gospel shows us the depth of his love and
compassion. God wants to be our heavenly Father.

Our problem is that we can believe God wants to save us,
but then will not look after us. We believe the gospel, but not
what it teaches us about God! It's illogical, but we think it
nonetheless. So consider Paul's words:

> He who did not spare his own Son, but gave him up for us all –
> how will he not also, along with him, graciously give us all things?
> (Romans 8:32)

This comes in a section speaking about our great security in
Christ. Paul's logic is simple. God hasn't spared his own Son.
Having given up so much for us, don't you think he will

continue to give us what we need? Don't you think God will continue to care for and protect us?

This does not mean that life will therefore be easy, not at all. As Paul goes on, he speaks about the hardships and suffering God's people might face. Paul himself faced such hardships, including a shortage of food. And yet he says that nothing will ever be able to separate us from the love of God that is in Christ Jesus our Lord (Romans 8:39).

So the gospel teaches us, firstly, that life is about relationship with God, and secondly, that God is utterly committed to us. These are powerful weapons with which to fight anxiety. We first persuade ourselves that the source of our anxiety is not the thing of ultimate importance that it claims to be, not what life is all about. Rather, it takes its rightful place below our relationship with God, and that is what we want to live for. We persuade ourselves secondly that God cares for us and will not let us go. So we are reassured that that ultimate relationship is secure, and that God will graciously give us whatever we need.

Peace in practice

So how shall we grow in peace? We've seen the beginnings of that already. Here are some practical steps.

First, *get in line with God's agenda*. In other words, in whatever anxiety-provoking situation you are in, seek first God's kingdom and righteousness.

I had been writing this chapter and then an email arrived. It detailed an angst-filled situation at church, which meant I needed to have a difficult conversation with someone. I spent the weekend with the issue constantly on my mind. I thought of all the ways in which that conversation might go. I imagined best-case and worst-case scenarios, and all their results. This is what anxiety does to us! Later I smiled ruefully and said to my wife, 'I spend the day writing about knowing God's peace, and then God gives me some homework!'

What should I do first? In such situations, my greatest concern can be about what people will think of me, what nasty consequences might result, or what I don't want to happen. That is what is driving my worry. Instead, I need to seek God's kingdom and his righteousness. I need to do the right thing before him and trust him for the consequences, do what will promote God's rule and not what is pragmatic or easiest, especially if it ducks the real issues. Remember, Jesus' call to peace doesn't just leave us unchanged; it reorientates us. We consciously need to bring that into play when we face anxiety.

Secondly, *we turn to God in prayer*. Consider Paul's words to the Philippians:

> Do not be anxious about anything, but in every situation, by prayer and petition, with thanksgiving, present your requests to God. And the peace of God, which transcends all understanding, will guard your hearts and your minds in Christ Jesus.
> (Philippians 4:6–7)

Anxiety usually drives us to mental action where we are thinking about the cause of our anxiety over and over again. We consider the possible outcomes; we imagine different scenarios; we lament getting into this situation in the first place. That is what I was doing with my church situation.

But Paul sees that the means to stopping our mental fretting is not calming ourselves down, or taking charge of our thoughts. Rather, the alternative to anxiety is *prayer*. Paul calls us to pray in 'every situation', and so not be anxious about 'anything'. All of our anxieties are to be dealt with by prayer.

Paul tells us to 'let our requests be known to God'. God knows our requests before we open our mouths, but this verse calls us to express our need of him in specific terms. We are to make requests: please stop this thing happening; please provide what we need; please bring help. We make these requests known by 'prayer and petition': speaking to God generally (prayer), but also by calling on him to do something (petition).

We call on God in this way 'with thanksgiving'. This cannot be a grumbling, complaining sort of prayer. Rather, it is a confident, trusting prayer. It knows God is our Father who cares, and is concerned for our good. It knows God has already provided so much for us, so it is thankful.

When I was faced with my church situation, the answer wasn't simply to block out my anxious thoughts or to distract myself. It was to think about my concerns, but to think about them *before* God. Rather than letting my anxieties run the show, I was to take them *to God*, to make requests and ask for action *from* God. I was to do so while humbly trusting his goodness and power, and being thankful for his care and provision. Pray like this yourself. Pray like this with, and for, others.

Thirdly, *we humble ourselves before God*. Here's what Peter says:

> Humble yourselves, therefore, under God's mighty hand, that he may lift you up in due time. Cast all your anxiety on him because he cares for you.
>
> (1 Peter 5:6–7)

It's the second sentence here that gets printed on Christian cards and calendars. It is a lovely verse: we can cast all our anxieties on God; every one of them can be thrown to him. We do this because we know he cares for us. It is a truth deserving of many calendars.

It's worth putting it together with the first sentence though. In fact, the two sentences run together: 'humble yourselves . . . casting all your anxiety'. The humbling of ourselves goes hand in hand with the casting of our anxiety. The logic runs like this: when we humble ourselves, we acknowledge God's greatness and our dependence. We think of him as the biggest, wisest and strongest dad in the world, and put our hand in his. We bow to his sovereign will rather than fighting against him.

Pride and worry go together, and so too do humility and peace.

The opposite, of course, is not to humble ourselves but to remain proud. That means we have big views of ourselves and small views of God. We need to take care! Pride and worry go together, and so too do humility and peace. This is why Thomas R. Schreiner says,

> Worry is a form of pride because when believers are filled with anxiety, they are convinced that they must solve all the problems in their lives in their own strength. The only god they trust in is themselves. When believers throw their worries upon God, they express their trust in his mighty hand, acknowledging that he is Lord and Sovereign over all of life.[2]

Wonderfully, God is not only the mighty sovereign; he is also the One 'who cares for you'.

So, with my anxiety-provoking situation at church, I needed to bow before God, to acknowledge that he was in charge and I wasn't. He was Lord over this situation, not me. I needed to recognize once again his bigness and my smallness, to remind myself that he cared deeply for me and everyone else involved.

I needed to know that he invited me to submit to him and cast my cares on him.

A word of encouragement

Think of the spectrum of anxiety mentioned earlier. Some of you will be fairly laid-back and not too troubled by anxiety. For others, anxiety is a daily struggle. Lots of factors play into why that is the case. But none of us is a complete stranger to worry.

Here's the important point. It's not how often or how easily we feel anxious, because if we think that's the issue, then some people will feel good about themselves and others will feel crushed. The real issue is what we do when anxiety strikes. There will be times of fear, times of worry. The question is: what do we do with them? Where do we turn?

Peter told us to cast our anxieties on God. He's assuming we will have some anxieties to cast. Paul told us to stop being anxious and start praying. He's assuming there's something worrying away inside us. But in both cases, our anxieties drive us to God, and so to know his peace.

King David said,

When I am afraid, I put my trust in you.
    In God, whose word I praise –
in God I trust and am not afraid.
    What can mere mortals do to me?
(Psalm 56:3–4)

5
humility

I once confessed to a friend that I struggled with pride. He replied that he was surprised to hear that, because he couldn't think of anything I had to be proud of! I should have known better than to be honest.

Unfortunately, the sad reality is that I don't actually need anything to be proud of in order to feel proud. It's not a condition that depends on reality; it's an attitude that just bubbles up within me. And I don't think I'm the only one. In different ways, and with different faces, we are all proud, and we all need to learn to be humble.

Pride and humility are heart attitudes to do with how we regard ourselves. More precisely, they are how we regard ourselves in relation to others. You lift yourself up over someone else in pride; you lower yourself below someone else in humility. The really scary thing is that we can be proud before God, whereas we should only ever be humble.

The dangers of pride

It is very easy in our culture to think that pride isn't really a big deal. We might find it a bit annoying in people, but it's not all that bad. In fact, some say it simply goes along with self-confidence and that it should even be encouraged. It is often linked to having a positive self-image, and children in particular are encouraged to have something to be proud of. There is a right place for satisfaction at doing something well, but in the Bible, pride is a dangerous thing. In fact, biblically speaking, 'pride is your greatest enemy and humility is your greatest friend'.[1]

> . . . those who exalt themselves will be humbled, and those who humble themselves will be exalted.
>
> (Luke 14:11)

Those words are from the lips of Jesus, but they echo a refrain that runs throughout the whole Bible. In pride, we exalt ourselves; we think more of ourselves than we ought to. Pride is a statement of our independence from God and a claim to our importance and significance aside from God. The minister and author John Stott defined pride like this:

> . . . the stubborn refusal to let God be God, with the corresponding ambition to take his place. It is the attempt to dethrone God and enthrone ourselves.[2]

That was what happened in the first sin. Adam and Eve in the Garden of Eden were tempted to become like God (Genesis 3:5). Rather than being content to be creatures, they wanted to lift themselves up and become like their Creator. Rather than being willing to live under God, they tried to exalt themselves above him. They were proud; they reached beyond themselves. And the result was that they fell.

God says he will bring down the proud. He stands against pride, because the proud stand against him. So we read in Proverbs:

> The LORD detests all the proud of heart.
>> Be sure of this: they will not go unpunished.
> (Proverbs 16:5)

See how God feels towards those who are proud? He detests them. This is pretty strong language. God hates those who are proud, and he will punish them. Pride is our greatest enemy.

Or see what God says he will do about pride in Isaiah:

> The LORD Almighty has a day in store
>> for all the proud and lofty,
> for all that is exalted
>> (and they will be humbled) . . .
> The arrogance of man will be brought low
>> and human pride humbled;
> the LORD alone will be exalted in that day,
>> and the idols will totally disappear.
> (Isaiah 2:12, 17–18)

God is allowing people to be proud. People can lift themselves up, and it looks like they are getting away with it. But Isaiah tells us that God has a day in store for them. He will humble people and exalt himself instead. Pride is perilous. A proud heart is set against God; it lifts itself up above him, but it won't stay there forever.

We all need to admit that we are tempted to be proud. It is part of our sin; it shapes our lives. Richard Baxter, a seventeenth-century minister, wrote these words about pride:

One of our most heinous and palpable sins is PRIDE . . .
it is so prevalent in some of us, that it directs our
discourses, it chooses our company, it forms our countenances,
it puts the accent and emphasis upon our words. It fills some
men's minds with aspiring desires, and designs. It possesses
them with envious and bitter thoughts against those who
stand in their light, or who by any means eclipse their
glory, or hinder the progress of their reputation. Oh what
a constant companion, what a tyrannical commander,
what a sly and subtle insinuating enemy, is this sin of
pride![3]

I don't know about you, but I know what he means. Pride
can so easily direct what I do and how I do it; what I say
and how I say it. Pride can fill my heart with dreams of
success and adulation. It can make me envious of others,
wanting to put them down and be seen to be better than
them. When I see this for what it is, I see pride is a nasty
piece of work. But as Baxter says, it is sly and subtle too;
every time I think I've got a handle on pride, it trips me
up again.

The safety of humility

By contrast to the great danger of pride, there is wonderful
safety in humility. As we read above, 'those who humble themselves will be exalted'. The humble understand their
dependence on God, see their need of him, recognize him as
King and bow before him. They don't try to lift themselves
up; they lower themselves down, and then he lifts them up
instead.

There are lots of Bible verses about how God regards those
who are humble. When you read them, you think to yourself
– this is a great way to be!

These are the ones I look on with favour:
    those who are humble and contrite in spirit,
    and who tremble at my word.
(Isaiah 66:2)

You save the humble
    but bring low those whose eyes are haughty.
(Psalm 18:27)

He guides the humble in what is right
    and teaches them his way.
(Psalm 25:9)

The LORD sustains the humble
    but casts the wicked to the ground.
(Psalm 147:6)

For the LORD takes delight in his people;
    he crowns the humble with victory.
(Psalm 149:4)

He mocks proud mockers
    but shows favour to the humble and oppressed.
(Proverbs 3:34)

Humility is the attitude that God is looking for.

We see a stark illustration of this in the Old Testament. God's people had been resisting him and rebelling against him. God finally decides to punish them. This comes in the form of the king of Egypt, called Shishak. He comes to the gates of Jerusalem to destroy the city. But see what happens next:

The leaders of Israel and the king humbled themselves and said, 'The LORD is just.'

> When the LORD saw that they humbled themselves, this word of
> the LORD came to Shemaiah: 'Since they have humbled themselves,
> I will not destroy them but will soon give them deliverance. My
> wrath will not be poured out on Jerusalem through Shishak.'
> (2 Chronicles 12:6–7)

The situation is like that where a parent is going to punish
their child for ongoing disobedience. But all that is needed is
for the child finally to recognize that they've done something
wrong, to admit that they deserve punishment and that their
parent is right. This then has an effect on the parent. All that
is required is humility.

Humility is what God wants from us.

What is humility?

We saw above that humility and pride work in relationships;
they are about how we view ourselves with regard to others.
So, humility is a right recognition of the relationship between
us and God: our smallness and his greatness. That recognition
flows from many different truths: God as Creator, us as
creatures; God as Provider, us as dependent; God as Saviour,
us as sinners. It is closely related to the 'fear of the Lord' which
we looked at earlier. In fact, one of the Proverbs joins the
two together:

> Humility is the fear of the LORD;
>   its wages are riches and honour and life.
> (Proverbs 22:4)

Humility is about our character, not our personality type or
temperament. It's not about being quiet. Humility doesn't
mean you can't know your own mind or be a strong leader –
after all, Moses was known as the most humble man of his day

(Numbers 12:3), and Jesus was the most humble person who ever lived. Humility is simply the right way to relate to God, an understanding of the reality of who he is and who we are.

Do you see the importance and significance of humility? Without it, we will not listen to or obey God, let alone worship him. Without humility, we will exalt ourselves and oppose God. Pride is our greatest enemy, and humility our greatest friend.

Pride is our greatest enemy, and humility our greatest friend.

A friend was once travelling in China. He saw a low doorway with a warning sign. In England, it would have said something like: 'Mind your head'. But the English translation of the Chinese original read: 'The lower, the safer'. That's a great summary of the Bible's view.

Humility: becoming a Christian

Here are some words from Jesus about entering his kingdom:

> At that time the disciples came to Jesus and asked, 'Who, then, is the greatest in the kingdom of heaven?'
>
> He called a little child to him, and placed the child among them. And he said: 'Truly I tell you, unless you change and become like little children, you will never enter the kingdom of heaven. Therefore, whoever takes the lowly position of this child is the greatest in the kingdom of heaven. And whoever welcomes one such child in my name welcomes me.'
> (Matthew 18:1–5)

Who's at the top of the ladder in the kingdom? How does Jesus answer? He doesn't say it's the person with the most faith, or the person who's most obedient, or the person who serves the most. Instead, he calls a little child and has him or her stand in front of them all. Then, he says the disciples need to 'change and become like little children'.

Jesus' words here have been debated. People have suggested he is pointing to the implicit trust or the supposed innocence of a child. But the question is about greatness. And the point is that in Jesus' day, children were considered 'leastest'. If you ranked people in society on a ladder, children were at the bottom. They had no rights or status. They were considered unimportant. So, when Jesus instructs his disciples to 'change and become like little children', he is saying, 'Lay down your own importance. Stop trying to rank yourself on the ladder, and place yourself at the bottom instead.'

In other words, the disciples' whole question was wrong. They asked, 'Who's the greatest in the kingdom?' Jesus said, 'Unless you turn from your concerns about greatness and humble yourselves, you won't even get into the kingdom.' You cannot hold onto your pride and status and self-importance, and become a Christian. It cannot happen; the two states are incompatible.

Here's another passage about humility and becoming a Christian:

> To some who were confident of their own righteousness and looked down on everyone else, Jesus told this parable: 'Two men went up to the temple to pray, one a Pharisee and the other a tax collector. The Pharisee stood by himself and prayed: "God, I thank you that I am not like other people – robbers, evildoers, adulterers – or even like this tax collector. I fast twice a week and give a tenth of all I get."
>
> 'But the tax collector stood at a distance. He would not even look up to heaven, but beat his breast and said, "God, have mercy on me, a sinner."

'I tell you that this man, rather than the other, went home justified before God. For all those who exalt themselves will be humbled, and those who humble themselves will be exalted.'
(Luke 18:9–14)

Do you notice to whom he is speaking? It is to those who are 'confident of their own righteousness and look down on everyone else', to people who are proud. So, Jesus tells the story of two people who go to pray: one proud, the other humble.

The Pharisee prays in a way that says, 'Thank you God that I'm so good; thank you that I'm not like people who sin all the time.' But the tax collector prays, 'I'm sorry God that I'm so bad; please have mercy on me.' Starkly contrasting attitudes: one regards himself highly, the other poorly. One thinks he has a claim on God; the other knows he doesn't. One looks down on others from a high position; the other places himself at the bottom of the pile.

Jesus finishes, 'I tell you that this man, rather than the other, went home justified before God.' That is, the tax collector went home right with God. Then comes that repeated refrain: 'For all those who exalt themselves will be humbled, and those who humble themselves will be exalted.'

The Pharisee was exalting himself – thinking of his supposed righteousness, and Jesus says that God will therefore bring him down. But the tax collector was humbling himself by admitting his sin, and Jesus says that God will therefore exalt him.

You can't become a Christian and hold your head up high at the same time. To become a Christian you have to say, 'I was wrong; I've rebelled; I need forgiveness.' You have to humble yourself, which is of course only recognizing reality, only seeing that we're not as great as we'd like to think we are, and that our rebellion against God is an awful thing. But when we do that, when we let go of our self-importance and pride, God himself lifts our head up, and we're made right with him.

I love the picture we see of this in the parable of the prodigal son (Luke 15:11–32). The son rebels against his father, and leaves home in proud, self-important independence. Later, when he realizes his sin, he returns home. But here's the point: he can't return *and* hold his head up high. No, he is rightly shamefaced, rightly falls on his knees before his father. He admits his sin.

> *You can't become a Christian and hold your head up high at the same time.*

That's a picture of us and God: we can only come to God on our knees.

But once the son has humbled himself, what happens? His father lifts him up and he is restored to being a son, with a ring on his finger and a robe on his back.

So, humility is key to becoming a Christian. It's not that God simply likes humble people – rather that when we recognize who he is, who we are and what we've done, we shall humble ourselves before him. This is why Richard Baxter said,

> Humility is not a mere ornament of a Christian, but an essential part of the new creature. It is a contradiction in terms to be a Christian and not humble.[4]

So, if you're not a Christian, Jesus calls you to humble yourself before God, asks you to see the awfulness of your sin and the great mercy of God. He then offers you the promise that those who humble themselves before him, he will exalt.

Those of us who are Christians must remember this is how we entered the kingdom.

Humility: living as a Christian

Humility is not only a defining attitude in turning to God, but an attitude we continue in as Christians. Back in Matthew 18, Jesus said,

> Therefore, whoever takes the lowly position of this child is the greatest in the kingdom of heaven. And whoever welcomes one such child in my name welcomes me.
> (Matthew 18:4–5)

So, humility is not just how you get into the kingdom, it defines greatness once you are in. We need to be clear in our minds though that Jesus is not saying there's a sneaky way of being great in the kingdom; he is not saying that if you are humble, then everyone will think you are brilliant! It's not some sort of trick to use in order to say, 'Look at me.' You see that idea in the hypothetical book title: *Humility and How I Achieved It*!

That's not what Jesus means at all. Instead, he's turning our ideas of greatness upside down. The whole point of being humble is that you're not even thinking about yourself. That's what defines greatness for Jesus. That's what he values: people laying aside their own importance and being completely humble.

And this is a real challenge for us. Here's my confession: I'd quite like to be known as a humble person. That is, as long as I am known to be such, as long as people admire me! In other words, it's just another outworking of my pride. The challenge to be humble is that in reality it's asking for people not to regard me at all.

But God calls his people to walk humbly with him (Micah 6:8). Humility is to shape our lives; it is part and parcel of life in the kingdom. We enter on our knees and we're to stay like that.

So let's unpack this attitude to God. First, an attitude of humility means we bow *in submission to* him. Peter says,

> 'God opposes the proud
>> but shows favour to the humble.'
> Humble yourselves, therefore, under God's mighty hand, that
> he may lift you up in due time.
> (1 Peter 5:5–6)

Peter is writing to people facing suffering. He's saying that they should have humility before God, accepting whatever situation they're in, whatever hardships they have to face. Humility goes hand in hand with submitting to God. It is the opposite of the attitude that says, God should change things; he doesn't know what he's doing. That's the voice of pride that thinks we know better than God.

An attitude of humility also means that we *take God's Word seriously.* Here's an example from Isaiah:

> These are the ones I look on with favour:
>> those who are humble and contrite in spirit,
>> and who tremble at my word.
> (Isaiah 66:2)

Humility before God is shown by trembling at his Word. If I have a big view of someone and remember how important and significant they are, then I will take what they say seriously. Just think how you react to the words of those 'above' you: the chairman of your company, the police or the captain of your sports team. You disregard their words at your peril; therefore you are attentive. Take that idea and magnify it! This is God speaking to you. If we see his greatness and our smallness, then we shall 'tremble at his Word'.

By contrast, pride is often seen in having a casual attitude to God's Word and rejecting what he says. We read about Zedekiah, a king in the Old Testament:

> He did evil in the eyes of the LORD his God and did not humble
> himself before Jeremiah the prophet, who spoke the word of
> the LORD.
> (2 Chronicles 36:12)

That attitude of pride and not listening leads us to the next element in humility: *obedience to God*. Zedekiah didn't listen, and so he did 'evil in the eyes of the LORD'. Throughout the Old Testament, when God's people repeatedly disobey, it is often linked to their heart attitude of pride. When God confronts them and calls them back to him, the question then is whether they will humble themselves before him and obey, or continue in proud rebellion. So, when God challenges his people through Jeremiah, he says this:

> To this day they have not humbled themselves or shown
> reverence, nor have they followed my law and the decrees I set
> before you and your ancestors.
> (Jeremiah 44:10)

The heart attitude of humility before God, and reverence for him, is shown in obedience to him. But sadly, in this verse, disobedience goes hand in hand with the absence of humility.

If you know you are disobeying God, turn back to him in humility. The letter of James is written to those who are double-minded in their relationship with God. They say they love him, but they also love the world. James says they are 'adulterous' as they are being unfaithful to God. James' call to them is to 'submit yourselves, then, to God' (James 4:7). The Old Testament verse he quotes to persuade them is this:

> God opposes the proud
>> but shows favour to the humble.
> (James 4:6)

So James calls his readers to turn back to God: 'Humble yourselves before the Lord, and he will lift you up' (James 4:10).

If you are resisting God in proud arrogance, please know that he will oppose you. But if you will submit to him, humble yourself before him, then he will pour his grace into your life and lift you up.

Lastly, humility goes hand in hand with *dependence in prayer*. Humble people call on God, knowing their weakness, their need of him, confessing their sins. For example, in the Old Testament, the Israelite king Manasseh was brought to realize his great sin, and he finally turned back to God. We're told:

> In his distress he sought the favour of the LORD his God and
> humbled himself greatly before the God of his ancestors.
> (2 Chronicles 33:12)

Manasseh's humility was shown in a prayer of confession. But we don't only express humility in prayer when we've sinned. Humility simply expresses our general dependence on God and need of him. For example, when Ezra set out on a significant journey back to Israel, we read:

> There, by the Ahava Canal, I proclaimed a fast, so that we might
> humble ourselves before our God and ask him for a safe journey
> for us and our children, with all our possessions.
> (Ezra 8:21)

Ezra showed his humility in praying for protection, knowing how weak and vulnerable he was. In prayer, we recognize the reality of our utter dependence on God. By contrast, a lack of prayer is very often a sign of pride.

So humility is seen in submission to God, taking his Word seriously, obeying him, and depending on him in prayer.

In all of these examples, we recognize that God is God, not me; he knows best; he's in control; he's the King. Humility then follows a clear view of God like a shadow. For if we see who God is, then humility will be there, sharp and defined. But when we lose sight of God, our view of ourselves starts to grow, humility evaporates and pride starts to increase.

A key verse for me in this context is from the book of Daniel. The Babylonian king Nebuchadnezzar had become proud. God taught him a lesson that showed him this. Afterwards, Nebuchadnezzar said these words:

> His dominion is an eternal dominion;
>   his kingdom endures from generation to generation.
> All the peoples of the earth
>   are regarded as nothing.
> He does as he pleases
>   with the powers of heaven
>   and the peoples of the earth.
> No one can hold back his hand
>   or say to him: 'What have you done?'
> (Daniel 4:34–35)

With that sort of picture of God, humility will inevitably follow.

In this book, we are focusing on heart attitudes in relationship with God rather than with each other. But let me quickly point out that humility before God is directly connected to humility towards one another. Jesus himself said so back in Matthew 18. Having spoken of entering the kingdom as a child, he went on:

> And whoever welcomes one such child in my name welcomes me.
> (Matthew 18:5)

Remember that children were considered insignificant in Jesus' day. So he is saying, 'Welcome insignificant people.' We too should welcome people whom others won't think are worthy of care. Do this because you are prepared to put yourself under everyone.

Jesus is saying that our attitude to 'insignificant' people reveals our attitude to him. Our attitudes towards other people provide a litmus test of our attitude towards God. If we think we are

'How can anyone be arrogant when he stands beside the cross?'

above welcoming insignificant people in Jesus' name, then we should be worried. We can't receive Jesus and be concerned about our own greatness at the same time.

Humility and the gospel

Carl Henry was a great church leader in the United States in the twentieth century. He was a brilliantly gifted man, well known as a writer, speaker and leader. But he was also known for his humility. Someone once asked him how he remained humble. He simply replied, 'How can anyone be arrogant when he stands beside the cross?'

How true that is.

We have many reasons to be humble. This is not our world, and we are not God in it. We are creatures utterly dependent upon our Creator. We are small and weak, and he is big and strong. We are powerless, and he is sovereign.

No-one can stand beside the cross and think proud thoughts.

But it is when we look at the cross of Jesus that we will be humbled beyond anything else. Once again, the gospel is the tool to use to teach our hearts to be humble. When we look at the cross, we're reminded of our sin, how appalling it is and what judgment it deserved. But we're also reminded of God's mercy, how gracious it is and how utterly underserved. No-one can stand beside the cross and think proud thoughts. In fact, you can hardly stand at all; you can only kneel and say thank you.

6
confidence

When my family is on holiday, we sometimes visit old church buildings. These are usually very grand and impressive – that's why they're highlighted on the tourist map. Very often there is an area at the front where the minister or the priest conducts the service. It's often up a few steps, sometimes roped off or with a rail running round it.

What's interesting is watching the attitude of tourists. They usually fall into two groups. The majority are *cautious*. They instinctively think that this area is special. Maybe they even think it is 'holy'. Only particular people are allowed in there. If a child starts to run across the space, you hear the parent's hissed commands: 'Come back!'; 'Get off there!'

The other group are less common. Rather than cautious, these people are *casual*. For them, this is like sauntering across the entrance lobby of their hotel. They wander into this space without so much as thinking about it. They smile at their children as they play there. As the cautious group cast anxious glances at them, the casual group wonder what people are staring at.

Of course, this part of a church building isn't special at all. But watching people's attitudes makes me think of our attitude towards God. How do we feel about coming before him? If we could walk into his presence, would it be with hesitant caution or with casual ease?

The good news of the gospel is that it should be neither. Rather, it should be with a heart attitude of *confidence*.

The old cautionary tale

That idea of a special area that is 'holy' comes from the Old Testament. God commanded that his people build a tabernacle, which was a type of tent. They were travelling around, and every time they set up camp, this tent was at the centre of their encampment. Once they were settled in the Promised Land, they eventually stopped using the tent and built a temple instead.

Both the tent and the temple pictured God's presence with his people. When God gave instructions about building the tabernacle, he said, 'Then let them make a sanctuary for me, and I will dwell among them' (Exodus 25:8). This was part of his covenant promise to them, that they would be his people and he would be their God (see Exodus 6:7). It was the promise of a relationship, and the tabernacle and the temple were tangible signs of that relationship. People could point to those structures and think, *God is living among us.*

The problem was that the tabernacle and then the temple also taught something else: that God's people couldn't get very close to him.

In the tabernacle there was an outer courtyard with an altar for offering sacrifices to God, and then a tent. In the tent there were two parts separated by a curtain. The first part was called the 'Holy Place'. It had an altar on which incense was burned. The second part, behind the curtain, was called the 'Holy of Holies'. It was the holiest place, in a holy place! In this section there was the 'ark of the covenant'. This symbolized God's actual presence. God said that above this ark was where he would meet with his people (Exodus 25:22). The layout changed slightly in the temple, but the basic idea remained the same.

The problem was that ordinary Israelites couldn't just wander into the tabernacle. Only the priests were allowed in, and they had to be consecrated with special sacrifices first (see Exodus 29). Even then, they had to wash themselves in a special basin each time they went in, 'so that they [would] not die' (Exodus 30:20). It was as if they needed a spiritual wash before they could come near God's presence.

But even the priests were not allowed into where God really dwelt – the Holy of Holies. Only one man, the high priest, was allowed in there, and this was only once a year on a special day, the Day of Atonement, and in order to do so, special sacrifices needed to be made (see Leviticus 16:3–6).

So the tabernacle and temple were wonderful signs of God's presence, but also worrying signs of limited access. God's holiness and people's sinfulness meant there was no place for casualness. In fact, casualness would get you killed. Even the high priest was told he would die if he entered the Holy of Holies whenever he liked (Leviticus 16:2). So, caution was the order of the day.

But that's not how God wanted it to be forever.

The new work of sacrifice

The book of Hebrews focuses on the work of Jesus through his death. It uses the categories of the Old Testament tabernacle and temple. In fact, chapter 9 begins with a description of how the tabernacle was set up. The author describes the rooms, and then he says,

> When everything had been arranged like this, the priests entered regularly into the outer room to carry on their ministry. But only the high priest entered the inner room, and that only once a year, and never without blood, which he offered for himself and for the sins the people had committed in ignorance.
> (Hebrews 9:6–7)

And that arrangement teaches us something:

> The Holy Spirit was showing by this that the way into the Most Holy Place had not yet been disclosed as long as the first tabernacle was still functioning.
> (Hebrews 9:8)

So, limited access taught that the way into God's presence hadn't yet been revealed. But the author assumes that God had always planned to reveal that new way. God didn't want to keep his people at a distance.

The central chapters of Hebrews then show how Jesus fulfilled the sacrifices of the Old Testament. The author refers to the annual sacrifice on the Day of Atonement, when the high priest offered a sacrifice in God's presence in the Holy of Holies.

But now we're told, 'Christ came as high priest', and rather than appearing before God in the man-made tabernacle, 'he went through the greater and more perfect tabernacle that is not made with human hands, that is to say, is not a part of this creation' (Hebrews 9:11). Later, we read that Christ 'entered heaven itself, now to appear for us in God's presence' (Hebrews 9:24).

So the Old Testament tent with the Holy of Holies was just a model for teaching us. Jesus is now the priest who appears before God the Father in heaven. This is the real deal.

But Jesus is not just the new high priest appearing before God. He is also the sacrifice:

> But he has appeared once for all at the culmination of the ages
> to do away with sin by the sacrifice of himself.
> (Hebrews 9:26)

This appearance 'once for all' is in contrast to the regular appearing of the Old Testament high priest who had to present himself every year to offer the sacrifice on the Day of Atonement. And the regular priests offered other sacrifices every day. That was because those sacrifices could never really deal with our sins. Actually, the fact that the sacrifice had to be offered again and again was a reminder of sins (Hebrews 10:3–4).

Here's an illustration: I presume you brush your teeth every day. Probably twice a day. You do so because they keep on getting dirty. Cleaning them is a daily task because the cleaning from yesterday doesn't continue into today. Unfortunately, that's what it was like with Old Testament sacrifices. The sacrifice from yesterday didn't carry over to the next day, so more sacrifices had to be offered. The very fact that sacrifices had to be made so regularly showed that the cleansing they provided was only temporary. They didn't really deal with the source of the problem.

But here's the great contrast:

> Day after day every priest stands and performs his religious
> duties; again and again he offers the same sacrifices, which can
> never take away sins. But when this priest had offered for all time
> one sacrifice for sins, he sat down at the right hand of God, and

since that time he waits for his enemies to be made his footstool.
For by one sacrifice he has made perfect for ever those who are
being made holy.
(Hebrews 10:11–14)

Jesus sat down because his work of sacrifice was done. He
only had to offer one sacrifice for sin. By that sacrifice, he made
people perfect. It deals with sins completely, so there is no
need for any more:

And where these have been forgiven, sacrifice for sin is no longer
necessary.
(Hebrews 10:18)

Permanent cleansing has been achieved.

New cleansing of conscience

This work of Jesus in sacrifice relates to our conscience. You
know that feeling of guilt we have for what we do wrong?
We might try to justify ourselves or shake it off, but we
often still have a sense of conviction; we know we are guilty.
That's our conscience at work telling us we've done something wrong.

Under the Old Testament system, that sense of conviction
could never really be dealt with: 'the gifts and sacrifices
being offered were not able to clear the conscience of the
worshipper' (Hebrews 9:9). This meant that the sacrifices
needed to be offered again and again. If they'd really dealt
with our guilt, they'd have stopped:

For this reason it [the law] can never, by the same sacrifices
repeated endlessly year after year, make perfect those who draw
near to worship. Otherwise, would they not have stopped being

offered? For the worshippers would have been cleansed once for all, and would no longer have <u>felt guilty for their sins.</u>
(Hebrews 10:1–2)

Again, the author sees the Old Testament sacrifices as achieving something, but never getting to the heart of the problem.

If you suffer from diabetes, one way it is managed is by regular injections of insulin. The injection covers over the problem for a while. But soon you'll need another. So the treatment manages the disease but never cures it. That's what the temple sacrifices were like. They managed the problem of sin, but they never dealt with the cause.

But Jesus' perfect sacrifice of himself presented in the heavenly temple is the real thing. He brings a cure that gets to the heart of the problem. It would be like needing no more insulin injections, because the diabetes has gone completely.

This is what the old sacrifices were pointing forward to. The new sacrifice of Jesus now brings a new level of cleansing. The Old Testament sacrifices were able to cleanse people 'outwardly', but how much better Jesus' sacrifice will be:

How much more, then, will the blood of Christ, who through the eternal Spirit offered himself unblemished to God, cleanse our consciences from acts that lead to death, so that we may serve the living God!
(Hebrews 9:14)

Think about how you feel when you know you've done something wrong against someone. The thought or sight of that person makes you feel guilty. What you need is for that offence to be dealt with, and removed, so that your conscience is cleared, so you can think of and see that person without those feelings, and live in relationship with them. All that we have done wrong, every wrong thought, word and action, is dealt with in Jesus, and our guilt is wiped away.

New access to God

Having explained all of this, the author of Hebrews finally draws his big conclusion. This forms the climax to the whole book:

> Therefore, brothers and sisters, since we have confidence to enter the Most Holy Place by the blood of Jesus, by a new and living way opened for us through the curtain, that is, his body, and since we have a great priest over the house of God . . .
> (Hebrews 10:19–21)

Remember that the 'Most Holy Place' is the inner sanctuary that only the high priest could enter once a year. But now we're being told that we can all go in. And with 'confidence' too! That means a sense of boldness and assurance. You can walk in knowing you're allowed to, rather than peeking round the corner, hesitant and unsure.

It is hard for us to appreciate this, but for a first-century Jewish Christian, it was mind-blowing. This most holy place was the one room they'd never even dreamed of entering. Now they could enter with confidence!

Notice the source of confidence, though. It is not due to us, but because of the blood of Jesus. He has opened up a 'new and living way' for us to get in, through his body. We've been given an 'all-access pass' in Jesus, our new 'great high priest'. There are no off-limits areas. We can get as close to God as we like.

My friend George is a university professor. He knows the principal of the university well; they are old friends. But even so, he would never simply wander into the principal's office without knocking or asking his secretary. So, said George, 'I have more confidence to walk into the throne room of God than I do to enter my principal's office.' You should have seen the smile on his face as he said it. He *knew* he could approach his Father with complete confidence, and that was fantastic.

We need to get hold of the fact that this confidence is ours personally. Notice how the author in Hebrews uses the word 'since'. He says, 'since we have' this confidence to enter, and 'since we have' this new high priest – he is assuming that these things are true and are ours.

Reflect:

- Do you believe you have Jesus as this new high priest?
- Do you believe you have this new access to God?
- Are you confident in this?

Our author is saying that these things are true, and since we have them, we can now live differently. There are then three things that he encourages us to do.

New closeness to God

First he says,

> . . . let us draw near to God with a sincere heart and with the full assurance that faith brings, having our hearts sprinkled to cleanse us from a guilty conscience and having our bodies washed with pure water.
> (Hebrews 10:22)

Jesus' work means we can draw near to God. But what does this mean? I think it is a mixture of an attitude and an action.

Think of a relationship with a friend or a spouse. What does it mean to 'draw close' to that person? It means first an *attitude* of focusing on them, having them at the centre of your attention, bringing them to the front of your mind. But it also means an *action* of speaking with them, spending time in their presence.

We can't draw close to God physically. Our relationship with him is through Jesus and by the Spirit. But there are similar attitudes and actions. Drawing close to God means focusing our thoughts on him, considering him and dwelling on him. It means coming to him in prayer, speaking with him, asking things of him, praising and thanking him.

Earlier in the book of Hebrews, the author said something similar:

> Let us then approach God's throne of grace with confidence, so that we may receive mercy and find grace to help us in our time of need.
> (Hebrews 4:16)

This is a parallel passage to Hebrews chapter 10, and it helps us understand this idea of drawing close. We are called to 'approach' God – that is, in our minds and hearts, we focus on him. We ask him for mercy and help; we speak to him; we pour out our hearts before him. As we do so, he strengthens us in our need. Notice again the attitude with which we can come: it is 'with confidence'.

The point the author is making is simple: we *can* draw close, so *let us do so*. Jesus has won us this new access.

Do you have confidence in approaching God? Many of us don't. Just consider some of the other phrases used in Hebrews 10 to imprint this confidence deep into our hearts. The author says that we can draw close to God like this in 'full assurance'. There need not be the slightest hint of caution, nor a moment of concern or worry.

Do you know that feeling of apprehension when you're not sure how someone will respond to you? You call over to them or phone them up, but you're not sure what reception you might get. You need never feel like that with God! Full assurance means total confidence.

A second phrase relates to our conscience again: we can draw near to God in full assurance, 'having our hearts sprinkled to cleanse us from a guilty conscience'. The times when we are most apprehensive over approaching other people are those times when we've done something wrong. If we feel guilty towards someone, then we will feel uncomfortable about approaching them. We'd even prefer to avoid them. We certainly wouldn't bound up to them and ask them a favour! In other words, you don't draw near to them.

Full assurance means total confidence.

But imagine that that person offers you forgiveness, and you know that the issue has been dealt with, truly done and dusted, in the past and left behind. Then you can draw near to them, come into their presence, talk to them, ask things of them and trust them.

That is what God offers us in Jesus. We can draw close to him, knowing our hearts are cleansed from their guilt. We come to him even when we feel guilty, knowing that as we do so, he freely forgives.

God wants us to realize the access he has gained through Jesus, and so to come close to him, not keep our distance. He wants us to come into that Holy Place where he is, to draw near in full assurance, knowing he's made that possible, knowing he wants us to be there.

Do you believe that? Do you believe that after you have sinned? When you know you have got things wrong? Do you really believe that God wants you to draw near with your conscience cleansed?

Do you believe that after you feel you have failed? After you have ignored God? Do you believe he wants you to come straight back, not hesitant and unsure, but confident of his welcome?

Do you believe that is true for everyone who believes in Jesus, no matter what they have done? Is it true for the sex offender, the adulterer, the alcoholic? Do you believe that no-one need stand further back from God, because of Jesus? Do you believe that you have a front-row invitation yourself?

God wants us to know the complete security and safety of this relationship he has created through Jesus. He wants us to be *confident*.

New hope to hold on to

We can draw near. But there is a second call:

> Let us hold unswervingly to the hope we profess, for he who promised is faithful.
> (Hebrews 10:23)

The encouragement is to 'hold unswervingly'. Picture grasping hold of a rope and keeping a tight grip, holding on and not being tempted to let go. That's what we're being called to do. The rope is the 'hope we profess'. That is our hope that this new relationship with God and access to him which will one day be fulfilled. The amazing thing is that the access we now have is the not the end game of God's plans. Jesus will return to bring his kingdom fully and finally. Our salvation will be complete, our relationship with God consummated and our faith rewarded.

The book of Hebrews often pictures the Christian life as being like a marathon. The author knows his readers are feeling weary and tired, feeling like giving up. So he does two things. He tells them about their relationship with God now: that they have this access to God now, that they can draw close to God now. But he also tells them to look ahead. This relationship with God is going somewhere. So he says, 'You don't have it all yet. The finishing line is coming. Hold on to your hope.'

It is a call to hang on and so press on. And he gives a reason: because 'he who promised is faithful'. God has said to us, 'I will do these things', and he keeps his promises. So we grip on to our hope as tightly as we can, like a lifeline, and do not let it go.

Two things can undermine any relationship. The first is feeling unsure of someone: unsure that they like us, how they'll act towards us, unsure of their view of us. If we are unsure of that, then the relationship is in trouble. But it's just as significant if we are not sure what they'll be like in the future. If we feel we can't trust them, then we won't trust ourselves to them. Hebrews is saying that we have this confident access to God now, and for the future; God is faithful and he won't change his mind.

Pressing on in the Christian life can be hard – we can be weary and feel like giving up. That is normal. What we need is the confidence of our relationship with God now, and confidence in his promises for the future.

New community to keep us going

The last implication comes with one more encouragement:

> And let us consider how we may spur one another on towards love and good deeds, not giving up meeting together, as some are in the habit of doing, but encouraging one another – and all the more as you see the Day approaching.
>
> (Hebrews 10:24–25)

This new relationship with God is corporate, not individual. We have access to him together, as his people. We can and must encourage one another in this relationship. Encouragement is a big theme in Hebrews. We're not talking about the sort of encouragement where we say, 'Well done, you're good at that.' Rather, encouragement in Hebrews means telling one another how good what God has done in Jesus is. It means telling each other how brilliant Jesus is, and the wonderful access to God we have through him. It means telling one another that God is faithful, and so encouraging one another to keep going in living for him.

Encouragement, then, strengthens us in our hold of the gospel.

The alternative is that we stop meeting together. Literally, it is that we 'forsake' or 'abandon' meeting with each other. And that spells disaster for the Christian, as the loner Christian is the un-encouraged Christian. As far as Hebrews is concerned, that's the Christian who will soon let go of their hope. In fact, there is no such thing as a strong individual Christian. It's a myth. We are all very weak and need one another to keep going – I know I do.

The strong Christian is only strong because they rely on the encouragement of others. We shouldn't neglect church because we think we are strong; rather we must go to be strengthened. We need one another to be spurred on. We need to meet so that we can be encouraged in this gospel confidence.

Confidence and the gospel

We saw at the start that some people thought about approaching God with hesitant caution, whereas others thought they could wander up with casual ease. Neither is true. We dare not be casual with God: the gospel teaches us that we are sinful and we cannot simply wander into his presence. The Old

Testament tabernacle taught us that loudly and clearly, and we must remind ourselves of that.

However, that does not mean that God wants us to be hesitant and unsure of him. The gospel also teaches us what he has done through Jesus, that we can have great confidence in approaching God, confidence in our whole relationship with him.

We're not casual because we know what it cost to gain us access. We know that Jesus' blood needed to be shed. But we can still approach God confidently, not confident in ourselves, nor in how well we've lived over the past few days, but confident in Jesus no matter how badly we've lived.

This is how the apostle Paul puts it:

> In him and through faith in him we may approach God with freedom and confidence.
> (Ephesians 3:12)

We desperately need to know this. I think of Susan. She was pressing on in her walk with God. She knew the gospel well. She had led Bible studies in her church and cared for people in her small group. She was a mature Christian, serving and active. But when asked about her relationship with God, she was hesitant and unsure.

She put it like this: 'If I think of how God must feel about me, I always feel like he's disappointed.' She would think of God as wearing a frown on his face. The result was caution and distance.

Susan needed to be assured of the gospel, to hear words like 'freedom', 'assurance' and 'confidence'. She needed to grow in the reality of those words, and to do so by applying the gospel to her heart, by knowing the work of Jesus more deeply, by being assured of God's welcome, and by hearing God's wonderful words of invitation: 'Let us draw near.'

God has thrown open the door and welcomed us in. He is for us, on our side! He has worked to bring us back to him. He wants us to come close, to know his welcome and his help. He wants us to be fully confident of that, and confident in him.

7
thankfulness

Our culture seems set to extinguish thankfulness. It pours cold water on it. There are several reasons for this.

Firstly, our culture is often cynical and sceptical. That lends itself to sarcasm rather than thankfulness. In fact, being thankful can come across as being rather naïve. It's as if someone who is smiling doesn't really understand what's going on around them. We wouldn't want to be seen like that, would we?

Secondly, our culture is driven by consumerism, which tells us that we need and deserve more. I went to the cinema recently, and at least two adverts before the film mentioned what we 'deserve'. One promised 'the future you deserve', and another offered 'the perfect house you deserve'. If we live life with a sense of needing and deserving more, then that undermines any feelings of thankfulness for what we already have.

Thirdly, our culture (and I speak for Britain here) is often grumbling. Whether it's about train times, queues or the government, there's usually something to complain about.

Grumbling is always so much easier than gratitude. Many more conversations begin with 'I'm so fed up about . . .' than 'I'm so grateful for . . .'

Of course, most people have moments of thankfulness. These are sometimes for good health, but usually only after a health scare. They might be for friendships, but usually only when life is hard and people have helped out. Perhaps the thankful moment is for a new job, but that's more likely after a period of unemployment. It's usually when we see the alternatives that we are grateful for what we already have. But it doesn't take long for that to become normal, and then we cease to be thankful and start to expect more.

There's another deeper issue with thankfulness and why our culture avoids it. We're rarely aware of it, but it's at work all the time. Thankfulness acknowledges someone. It means someone has been kind and given what you don't deserve. It sees something as a gift.

There is a crucial difference between *being thankful* and *being glad*. We are glad about things or situations, but we are thankful to people. Gladness enjoys the goodness of something, but thankfulness acknowledges dependence upon a giver. That takes us to the heart of the biblical picture of thankfulness.

Being thankful
We'll start by looking at Psalm 136. Here's how it begins:

Give thanks to the LORD, for he is good.
   His love endures for ever.
Give thanks to the God of gods.
   His love endures for ever.
Give thanks to the Lord of lords:
   His love endures for ever.
(Psalm 136:1–3)

This psalm is a call to be thankful. Specifically, it's a call to give thanks to God. The reason? It's there right at the start: we give thanks 'for he is good'. That goodness is shown specifically in the next line, which is repeated all the way through the psalm: 'His love endures for ever.'

The word used for 'love' here is significant. It is the word for God's faithful covenant love, the love linked to his covenant promises to save his people. That love will endure forever. Our thankfulness is because of God's goodness, shown in his faithful, never-ending love.

The middle portion of the psalm then lists ways in which God has shown this love. It divides into two sections. First, there is creation:

> . . . to him who alone does great wonders,
> *His love endures for ever.*
> who by his understanding made the heavens,
> *His love endures for ever.*
> who spread out the earth upon the waters,
> *His love endures for ever.*
> who made the great lights –
> *His love endures for ever.*
> the sun to govern the day,
> *His love endures for ever.*
> the moon and stars to govern the night;
> *His love endures for ever.*
> (Psalm 136:4–9)

[handwritten annotation: brace beside verses labelled "Nature"]

Then we move to the salvation that God worked for his people in rescuing them from Egypt:

> . . . to him who struck down the firstborn of Egypt
> *His love endures for ever.*

and brought Israel out from among them
His love endures for ever.
with a mighty hand and outstretched arm;
His love endures for ever.
to him who divided the Red Sea asunder
His love endures for ever.
and brought Israel through the midst of it,
His love endures for ever.
but swept Pharaoh and his army into the Red Sea;
His love endures for ever.
to him who led his people through the wilderness;
His love endures for ever.
(Psalm 136:10–16)

Egypt

This psalm gives thanks for rescue from slavery in Egypt and conquest of their enemies. But that wasn't the end of their salvation. God then gave them victories in battle so that his people could enter the land he had promised where he would live with them. This too was part of his ongoing love for them:

. . . to him who struck down great kings,
His love endures for ever.
and killed mighty kings –
His love endures for ever.
Sihon king of the Amorites
His love endures for ever.
and Og king of Bashan –
His love endures for ever.
and gave their land as an inheritance,
His love endures for ever.
an inheritance to his servant Israel.
His love endures for ever.
(Psalm 136:17–22)

Battle

The psalm finishes as it began, with a call to 'give thanks to the God of heaven; his love endures for ever'.

Thankfulness: saying more than you think

Notice from this psalm that thankfulness involves two elements. Firstly, there is *acknowledging God's love*. The psalmist is saying that God has been good and kind and loving to them in these ways. As we indicated above, this is how thankfulness is different from gladness or joy. Joy is our delight in the thing we're given, in the gift; thankfulness is our attitude to the giver, acknowledging their goodness to us. So we're called to give thanks *to* the Lord.

Secondly, thankfulness is *acknowledging our dependence* on that person. If the people had been able to do these things for themselves, then they wouldn't have been very grateful. We are most grateful when someone does something for us that we desperately needed and that we couldn't have done without them.

If someone makes you a cup of tea, you say thank you, but you know you could have got the tea yourself, and you know you could have lived without it! We say thank you – and so we should – but it's not deep heartfelt gratitude. Deeply felt thankfulness acknowledges that we *needed* the other person. It says, 'I couldn't have done that without you.'

So Psalm 136 acknowledges God's goodness in creation, in rescue and the gift of the Promised Land. People are called to say thank you and acknowledge him: 'We couldn't have done that ourselves; we needed you.'

This is why thankfulness often merges with the idea of praise and worship. Here are a few examples:

I will give to the LORD the thanks due to his righteousness;
　I will sing the praises of the name of the LORD Most High.
(Psalm 7:17)

I will praise God's name in song
   and glorify him with thanksgiving.
(Psalm 69:30)

I will praise you, Lord my God, with all my heart;
   I will glorify your name for ever.
(Psalm 86:12)

Each of these verses is about giving thanks to God. But that flows into praising him, making much of him, exalting him. Thankfulness acknowledges him for what he has done for us.

Thankfulness: more significant than you think

We see the significance of thankfulness even more clearly if we consider its opposite. In the Bible, ingratitude is not simply forgetting to say thank you, and not just bad manners. In fact, it's a key element in sin. Here is how the apostle Paul describes mankind's fall into sin:

For although they knew God, they neither glorified him as God
nor gave thanks to him, but their thinking became futile and their
foolish hearts were darkened.
(Romans 1:21)

The dynamic of sin involves not glorifying God as we should, *and* not giving thanks to him. Sin means not acknowledging God's goodness to us and our dependence on him. Think back to Adam and Eve in the Garden of Eden. If they had been thankful to God, then they would not have turned against him.

> *The dynamic of sin involves not glorifying God as we should, and not giving thanks to him.*

There is a stark warning to us too from the history of God's people in the Old Testament. This history can be written in terms of the people's thankfulness, or lack of. So often they were ungrateful. Even after God had rescued them from Egypt and was leading them to the Promised Land, they started grumbling rather than being grateful (see Exodus 17:1–7). The result was a lack of trust in God, and finally rebellion against him.

Thankfulness is acknowledging God's goodness to us and our need of him; the opposite is independence from him and turning against him.

Thankfulness: more normal than you think

Psalm 136 was a call to God's people to be thankful, to give thanks for God's goodness and never-ending love. That was to be normal life for them. There would be special moments of thankfulness over particular events like victory in battle, good harvests, and more. But thankfulness wasn't to be limited only to those moments. Thankfulness was to be an ongoing, normal, everyday heart attitude.

The repeated refrain in that psalm – 'give thanks to the LORD, his love endures for ever' – was to be sung in the temple every day. David appointed priests to praise God in this way:

> He appointed some of the Levites to minister before the ark of the LORD, to extol, thank, and praise the LORD, the God of Israel. (1 Chronicles 16:4)

He gave them a song to sing which thanked him for all his goodness to them. It finished like this:

> Give thanks to the LORD, for he is good;
> his love endures for ever.

Cry out, 'Save us, God our Saviour;
    gather us and deliver us from the nations,
that we may give thanks to your holy name,
    and glory in your praise.'
Praise be to the LORD, the God of Israel,
    from everlasting to everlasting.
(1 Chronicles 16:34–36)

Thankfulness was to be the background music to all of
life.

We see the same call for ongoing thankfulness in the New
Testament. Paul writes to the Christians in Ephesus:

Sing and make music from your heart to the Lord, always giving
thanks to God the Father for everything, in the name of our Lord
Jesus Christ.
(Ephesians 5:19–20)

Notice again the link between thankfulness and praising God
in song. But note the phrase: 'always giving thanks'. It is a call
for ongoing gratitude.

Paul says here that we should be always giving thanks
'for everything'. That phrase has sometimes been misunderstood, as if Paul is telling us to give thanks for everything that happens in life. But I don't think he means that we should thank God for things that are bad, evil or downright wrong. In the context of the letter, I think it is about thanking God for everything he is doing, everything he gives us.

Thankfulness was to be the background music to all of life.

However, we are certainly to give thanks in all circumstances. Paul puts it like this:

> Rejoice always, pray continually, give thanks in all circumstances; for this is God's will for you in Christ Jesus.
> (1 Thessalonians 5:16)

So there is no time, no place, where the Christian does not give thanks. Similarly, in his letter to the Colossian church, Paul speaks of Christians as those who are 'overflowing with thankfulness' (Colossians 2:7).

So, thankfulness is part of normal Christian living. All right, we might not have people singing in a temple every day like in the Old Testament, but

Thankfulness is part of normal Christian living.

thankfulness should still be the background music in the life of the Christian. We might be upset or happy; life might be easy or hard; I might face joys or sorrows; but that music of thankfulness is always to be playing. We are continually to acknowledge God's goodness to us and our dependence on him.

Just as in Psalm 136, we give thanks like this in two areas.

God's goodness to us in creation

We read earlier about giving thanks to God who created the heavens, the earth and us. So we are thankful to him in acknowledging the very existence of this world and our own presence in it. We owe ourselves to him.

But we also acknowledge God's goodness through his provision in creation. A later verse says,

He gives food to every creature.
　His love endures for ever.
(Psalm 136:25)

God is our Creator and provider. He sends rain and sun, and
makes food grows. This is why Christians have traditionally
said thank you before meals. Jesus himself gave thanks before
he ate, acknowledging that this was what God had provided.
This is a truth that Paul tried to convince people of in evangel-
ism. In Acts, he said to people from an idol-worshipping
background,

> Yet he has not left himself without testimony: he has shown
> kindness by giving you rain from heaven and crops in their seasons;
> he provides you with plenty of food and fills your hearts with joy.
> (Acts 14:17)

Later, in Athens, Paul says,

> The God who made the world and everything in it is the Lord
> of heaven and earth and does not live in temples built by human
> hands. And he is not served by human hands, as if he needed
> anything. Rather, he himself gives everyone life and breath and
> everything else.
> (Acts 17:24–25)

God is the One who gives us everything we have in this world.
He is the dynamic behind the world's existence, preservation
and life. He is the great 'Giver', of life and breath, of food, of
joy. Indeed, any and every good thing we have is ultimately
from him.

This is crucial in how we handle good things today.
Thanksgiving is the key heart attitude that will prevent us

from either <u>demeaning good things</u> or <u>worshipping them</u>. We see this when Paul speaks about false teachers in 1 Timothy:

> They forbid people to marry and order them to abstain from
> certain foods, which God created to be received with
> thanksgiving by those who believe and who know the truth.
> For everything God created is good, and nothing is to be rejected
> if it is received with thanksgiving.
> (1 Timothy 4:3–4)

The issues here are marriage and food. These false teachers were trying to say that it would be more spiritual to abstain from these parts of creation. They disparaged these and said, 'Let's go without.' But Paul responds by saying that everything God created is good: marriage, food. We could continue the list: sport, art, music and so on.

So Paul says that nothing is to be rejected if it is received with thanksgiving. And receiving something with thanksgiving says two things about what is given. Firstly, it says it is a good thing, something to be grateful for. Secondly, it says it has come from God, a gift from him. Thanksgiving acknowledges the goodness of God's gift, and that he is the Giver.

We need to learn to see such gifts as good things. Some Christians have tended to be dismissive of what is good in creation, thinking that only 'spiritual' things matter. They need to learn the first step here: acknowledge that these are indeed good things.

However, that's not the most common problem. Speaking personally, I've never had a problem enjoying a good cup of coffee, a great game of football, a beautiful view and much, much more. My problem is that I tend to just accept it as what's there, what's normal. I'm glad about it, but I don't give

Thankful not Just glad

thanks for it. So I've had to learn to look at such things and say to myself, 'This is a gift from God, so I give thanks to him.' That second step is much more commonly needed today. We must stop looking at the world as an automatic vending machine that provides us with good things. This means looking at our marriages, our friendships, our jobs, our hobbies, and, despite the fact that not all of what we see will be enjoyable, giving thanks for what is good.

Thankfulness then comes about in part by a new way of looking at the world. It is utterly different from our culture and from what will be instinctive to us. We see all that is good as a gift from God. And we say thank you.

Try ending each day by thanking God for everything good that you enjoyed. Acknowledge his goodness and your dependence on him.

God's goodness to us in salvation

Psalm 136 also showed us thankfulness over salvation. God's people were slaves in Egypt, but God liberated them and brought them into the Promised Land. This is part of a huge theme in the Old Testament of looking back, remembering what God has done, and giving thanks.

Here's another example from the Psalms:

Give thanks to the Lord, for he is good;
    his love endures for ever.
Let the redeemed of the Lord tell their story –
    those he redeemed from the hand of the foe,
those he gathered from the lands,
    from east and west, from north and south.
(Psalm 107:1–3)

This psalm carries on speaking about all the ways in which

God has rescued people. They are to look back at what he has done in rescuing them, and give thanks.

Here's another example:

> I will give thanks to you, LORD, with all my heart;
> I will tell of all your wonderful deeds.
> (Psalm 9:1)

Again, the psalm looks back on all the 'wonderful deeds' which God has done, and gives thanks for them.

It's the same in the New Testament. Paul prays that God will be at work in the Colossian Christians, so they will be those who are

> . . . giving joyful thanks to the Father, who has qualified you to share in the inheritance of his holy people in the kingdom of light. For he has rescued us from the dominion of darkness and brought us into the kingdom of the Son he loves, in whom we have redemption, the forgiveness of sins.
> (Colossians 1:12–14)

Notice how this picks up on the Exodus picture from the Old Testament. Where were we? In the 'dominion of darkness', slaves to sin and Satan. What did God do? He 'rescued us'. Where did he bring us? Into 'the kingdom of the Son he loves', the kingdom of Jesus. He has qualified us to share in 'the inheritance of his holy people in the kingdom of light'. We look forward to being in that kingdom, where all is good.

It is these truths that lead Paul to pray that the Colossians will give 'joyful thanks'.

Thankfulness and the gospel

Thankfulness, then, has to do with realizing what God has

done for us in the gospel. We look back and remember, and we are filled with gratitude. I saw a helpful illustration of this on a recent holiday in Normandy. My boys love World War 2 history, and so we visited lots of historic sites there. The towns and villages had been under German Nazi occupation for many years, with the people living under a rule that was oppressive and restrictive. Then, following D-Day, the Allies brought liberation.

As we visited the museums and towns, I was struck by two things. First, the pictures of liberation. Everyone was so happy! There were parties everywhere: people rejoicing, hugging the liberating soldiers, handing out beer and wine.

The second thing was the way that liberation was remembered. There were cemeteries everywhere, annual celebrations and parades, monuments in every village. Everyone wanted to remember those who had brought liberation. You cannot travel far in Normandy without being reminded of its history.

If we are Christians, we too need to remember. We have been liberated from the kingdom of darkness, at the cost of God's own Son. We need to look back and remember how God has been good to us. That was what Psalm 136 was doing. Just think, that psalm didn't teach anything new. Everyone knew how God had rescued them – but they needed to sing it anyway to remind themselves, celebrate and give thanks.

Psalm 136 is about the Old Testament rescue from Egypt. If we wrote a New Testament equivalent, it would go something like this:

God so loved us that he sent his only Son,
   His love endures for ever.
Jesus, became a man for our sake.
   His love endures for ever.

He lived a perfect life of obedience for us.

His love endures for ever.

He suffered and died in our place.

His love endures for ever.

He bore the wrath of God to bring us forgiveness.

His love endures for ever.

He rescued us from slavery to sin.

His love endures for ever.

He defeated Satan and triumphed over him.

His love endures for ever.

He's brought us to know God as Father.

His love endures for ever.

He's promised us a great inheritance in his new creation.

His love endures for ever.

This is what we do when we sing about the gospel. We remind ourselves of these truths, and as we remember, we say thank you.

This is also what we are doing when we take the Lord's Supper together. God knew that we have this incredible ability to forget, not so much the facts – we don't forget that Jesus died for us – but to forget the significance. We forget God's mercy, goodness and love. So he told us to eat bread and drink wine 'in remembrance' of him; as we eat and drink, we 'proclaim the Lord's death' (1 Corinthians 11:23–26). We tell ourselves the gospel again, tell each other the gospel again, and we are thankful.

The call to be thankful

Let's finish this heart attitude with that call to be thankful:

. . . give thanks in all circumstances; for this is God's will for you in Christ Jesus.

(1 Thessalonians 5:18)

God calls you to be a thankful person; he calls your church to be a thankful church.

It is right to be thankful because God has been, and is, good to us, and we are dependent on him. Thankfulness only recognizes what is true. When God is limited in his goodness, then we can be limited in our thankfulness. When he has stopped faithfully loving us, then we can stop giving thanks. But this will never happen.

Being thankful then drives so much of the Christian life. If we are those giving thanks to God in all circumstances, then it's:

- harder to be proud
- harder to be cynical or bitter
- harder to be demanding
- harder to be greedy or envious
- almost impossible to feel hopeless
- easier to forgive
- easier to show kindness to others
- easier to stop focusing on our problems
- easier to make sacrifices

We will not fit into a culture that is cynical and sceptical – we may even stick out like a sore thumb. We will not fit in with the call to want more and feel we deserve more. We will be more likely to be grateful than to grumble. In such ways, we will stand out and give testimony to God.

Here's a traditional prayer on thankfulness. Why not make this your prayer too?

Almighty God, Father of all mercies, we your unworthy servants do give you our most humble and heartfelt thanks for all your goodness and loving-kindness to us and to all people.

We thank you for our creation, preservation, and all the blessings of this life; but above all for your incomparable love in the redemption of the world by our Lord Jesus Christ, for the means of grace, and for the hope of glory.

And we pray, please give us an awareness of all your mercies, that our hearts may be sincerely thankful, and that we show forth your praise, not only with our lips, but in our lives; by giving up ourselves to your service, and by walking before you in holiness and righteousness all our days; through Jesus Christ our Lord, to whom with you and the Holy Spirit be all honour and glory, for ever and ever. Amen.[1]

8
contentment

Try finishing this sentence: 'I would be content if . . .'

Or think of some friends and how they might answer it.

There are a variety of answers. They will inevitably relate to our current situation and what we are discontented with. They will also reveal where we think the 'answer' lies.

Some people think they would be content if they won the lottery, while others are looking for a regular income. Some people think they'd be content if they had a bigger house, while others would be happy with any house at all. Some would be content if they were healthy, usually because they are suffering from a disease at the moment. Some people think they'd be content if they had a new TV, a different job, a fabulous holiday or better looks. Others would look for relationships: friendships, romance or marriage. Some want children. Some want success, while others just want acceptance.

Right and wrong contentment

The first thing we need to do is to examine that list. Some of it reflects what has gone wrong with the world. When someone says they might be content if they were healthy, there is truth and validity in that because God didn't make us to live with sick bodies. Some people are discontent because of family breakdown, unemployment, singleness or childlessness. These can be part and parcel of living in a fallen world.

To put it differently, one source of discontentment is *because of suffering*.

At least part of that discontentment is right, because God didn't make us to live like that. All of us, whoever we are, in different ways, experience part of the suffering of living in a fallen world, and we feel like it shouldn't be like this. And that's true; it shouldn't.

I don't think the Bible uses the word 'contentment' in those situations. For example, in Romans 8, the apostle Paul speaks about our groaning in suffering, and our longing for the future new creation where such suffering will be gone. He says that such groaning and longing is good and right. There are many things to cry over in this broken world, and we will continue to cry until God wipes away every tear from our eyes (Revelation 21:4). We shall not be (and indeed we should not be) content about such things until the new creation.

Now, there is still a great challenge to us in those situations. We are to continue to trust God and his goodness, to know that he is even using such things for our good (Romans 8:28). There is the challenge of rejoicing within trials, or being at peace within suffering; these are heart attitudes that we looked at earlier. But even with those challenges, there is still a sense in which a Christian should not be content, because we know they are not how God meant the world to be.

As we think about the heart attitude of contentment, this is a crucial point to clarify. God calls us to be content, and so challenges our discontentment. But what he challenges is not discontentment over suffering, but over *wanting more*.

Always wanting more

Do you know how adverts work? They try to do two things. In the first place they try to persuade you that a product is worth having, that it will bring some new happiness, fun or satisfaction into your life. But they will also try to make you feel discontented. Advertisers want you to feel you *need* their product, so they make you think life isn't good enough as it is. The two aims are entwined: your discontentment will be solved by the product. Adverts create discontentment and then promise to solve it. So, in the world of advertising, you will never have enough.

My friend Sam once looked through a series of adverts and asked himself what was being promised through each product. The list included: power, peace, happiness, better family life, freedom, fun, comfort, friendship, success, identity, security, inspiration, harmony and insight. All of these were presented as making your life 'better'.

That list was for buying: a mobile phone, holidays, finance packages, footwear, a certain brand of tea, and other more mundane items! Of course, we all know that drinking a certain kind of tea or wearing new trainers doesn't change your family life or income. Adverts work by association and suggestion. But the point is that they do work.

It's not just adverts that create discontentment, though. Our culture creates the longing for a certain lifestyle, looks, success, a career, relationships, and more. This is conveyed through films, magazine articles, reality TV shows, blogs and novels.

But we don't even need our culture to develop such feelings of discontentment. It is all too easily the instinctive pull of our hearts that's responsible. I just have to look at my neighbour's extension and I feel dissatisfied with my own house. I only need to hear that a friend has been promoted in order to feel unhappy with my career. Adverts and our culture help us along, but we can feel discontented all by ourselves.

The danger for Christians, then, is that we can live life with hearts that always long for more. This may or may not show up on the shopping bill. It may or may not get worked out in how we spend our time, but it is lurking there in our hearts.

So here's our question: how do we live contented lives in a discontented culture? How can we be content in a world that constantly tells us we'll only be happy with more? Let's look at Paul's letter to Timothy. There are two key things to note.

Realize that wanting more is dangerous

Here's what Paul says:

> Those who want to get rich fall into temptation and a trap and into many foolish and harmful desires that plunge people into ruin and destruction. For the love of money is a root of all kinds of evil. Some people, eager for money, have wandered from the faith and pierced themselves with many griefs.
> (1 Timothy 6:9–10)

Paul is talking about the person who wants to be rich. It has to do with money, but the basic idea is someone who wants to have more. Paul points out the results for people with such an attitude.

Firstly, they fall into 'temptation'. They have opened themselves up to being enticed to sin. It is like the person on a diet choosing to walk down the chocolate aisle at the supermarket.

That is to place yourself in a dangerous situation of temptation. So, the person whose heart wants more has fallen into a dangerous place, where they will be tempted to sin.

Secondly, they fall into a 'trap'. It's like an animal being tempted by tasty meat, which really is the bait of a poacher. The word 'trap' was used earlier in the letter, referring to the 'devil's trap' (1 Timothy 3:7; also in 2 Timothy 2:26). So, it's most likely that this is a trap laid by Satan. He knows that getting people to want more and more is a great place to have them. If he can create discontentment and a longing for money and possessions, then we have fallen into his trap.

Thirdly, people fall into 'many foolish and harmful desires'. The longing for more money opens up a world of cravings.

Wanting more is a dangerous game to play.

The person who wants to be rich so often wants success and power too. They start comparing themselves with, and wanting to be richer than, their neighbour. There are knock-on effects on their friendships and their marriage too. But these desires are 'foolish and harmful'; they will do us damage.

The final result, says Paul, is that we are plunged into 'ruin and destruction'. The picture is of drowning. But we are drowning in ruin and destruction – physical and spiritual.

So, the desire for more is dangerous. It leads us down a road into temptation, the devil's trap and deadly desires. At the end of the road is destruction.

Wanting more is a dangerous game to play. We are playing with fire.

Loving money
The reason for such danger is explained in the next verse:

'For the love of money is a root of all kinds of evil' (1 Timothy 6:10).

This verse has been regularly misquoted in two ways. Firstly, it is sometimes quoted as: 'money is the root . . .'. However, it's not money itself, but the *love* of money. There's nothing wrong or evil about money and possessions in themselves; it's our attitude that is the problem. Secondly, it's often quoted as 'the love of money is the root of *all* evil' – as if it is responsible for everything that is wrong. But that's not what the verse says. There are lots of sources of evil, and love of money takes its place as one of them, not the only one.

But what the text does say is challenging enough. The love of money in our hearts produces all kinds of unsavoury fruit in our lives. It results in selfishness and materialism. It sees people as a means to an end. It thinks of life only in terms of financial gain. It can result in cheating and lying. It distorts family life and relationships.

Paul goes on to say that some people who are eager for money 'have wandered from the faith and pierced themselves with many griefs'. Loving money can lead you away from trusting Jesus and cause you to start to stab yourself – you are pierced by many griefs.

I think of the man whose love of money meant he spent long hours in the office. He saw his wife and children at weekends – but not even very much then. As his marriage gradually fell apart, and as his children became increasingly distanced from him, he realized he'd inflicted wounds on himself. Wanting more can wreck your life.

Or I think of the woman whose love of money meant that she obsessed about possessions. Life was all about what she had, how new it was and how it compared to everyone else's possessions. This became the theme of her life. The effects were more subtle, but they were still there: shallowness in relationships, always assessing people as competitors, telling little lies.

But the most worrying element of all of this is the spiritual destruction it can bring. In the parable of the sower, Jesus talks about the way we can hear his message. He associates different responses with different types of ground, and one response is described as ground with thorns in it. He says,

> Still others, like seed sown among thorns, hear the word;
> but the worries of this life, the deceitfulness of wealth and the
> desires for other things come in and choke the word, making
> it unfruitful.
> (Mark 4:18–19)

The picture is that of a fruitful response to God being choked off. What's doing the choking? It's the worries of this life, the deceitfulness of wealth and the desire for other things. Notice that Jesus says wealth is deceitful – it tricks you. It promises one thing, but delivers another. It promises happiness, fun and contentment, but it's all lies.

Paul wants to warn us against that desire for more which is so dangerous. Do you need to hear that warning today? What is your attitude to money? Do you love it? What are the telltale signs? Ask yourself:

- Do you daydream about having more money, more possessions?
- Are you overly worried about your finances?
- Do you think that more money will make life better?
- Do you compare yourself to others and wish you had more?

Instead of such danger, Paul encourages us to be content.

Realize that contentment is brilliant

Here are some earlier verses from our passage in 1 Timothy:

> But godliness with contentment is great gain. For we brought
> nothing into the world, and we can take nothing out of it. But
> if we have food and clothing, we will be content with that.
> (1 Timothy 6:6–8)

Paul has been talking about people who think that religion is
a way to financial success. The previous verse speaks about
those who 'think that godliness is a means to financial gain'
(verse 5). By 'godliness', he doesn't mean simply living a godly
life; it's a much broader idea. It's our relationship with God,
and living out that relationship. Some people, says Paul, think
that such a relationship is a source of money. We don't know
exactly how. They may have charged for religious instruction,
or they might have thought that God gave blessing in the form
of finances – like prosperity teaching often does today.

But whatever the reason, Paul turns it on its head and says: godliness is indeed a source of great gain. It is a brilliant thing. But,
notice, it is godliness *with contentment*. And it is not financial gain
he is talking about. He explains what he means: 'For we brought
nothing into the world, and we can take nothing out of it.'

We arrive and leave with no money, no possessions, no
chequebook, no valuables. We bring nothing with us, and we
take nothing with us. Paul is probably thinking of a verse back
in the Old Testament in the book of Ecclesiastes:

> Everyone comes naked from their mother's womb,
>   and as everyone comes, so they depart.
> They take nothing from their toil
>   that they can carry in their hands.
> (Ecclesiastes 5:15)

Remember the classic question at the funeral of a rich person: how much did they leave? The answer is: everything. We leave as we arrive. That says it all.

Do you know the board game 'The Game of Life'? As you play, you live your life, making decisions about education and career. It finishes with everyone adding up how much money they have. The person with the most wins. That demonstrates how our culture often thinks. But it's not true in real life. The meaning of life is nothing to do with money.

So, says Paul, 'If we have food and clothing, we will be content with that.' He knows we need a certain amount to live: food, appropriate nourishment, clothing and shelter (it includes the idea of a house to live in, as well as clothes to wear). But if life is not about how much we have, then if we have enough of those things, we'll be content.

Now, this doesn't mean that Paul wants us to despise money or possessions, for a little later he says this:

> Command those who are rich in this present world not to be arrogant nor to put their hope in wealth, which is so uncertain, but to put their hope in God, who richly provides us with everything for our enjoyment. Command them to do good, to be rich in good deeds, and to be generous and willing to share. In this way they will lay up treasure for themselves as a firm foundation for the coming age, so that they may take hold of the life that is truly life.
> (1 Timothy 6:17–19)

Those who are rich must not be proud, or place their confidence in their money. That would be a terrible place to put your trust – as stock market crashes and recessions keep on showing us. Instead, says Paul, they must put their hope in God 'who richly provides us with everything for our enjoyment'.

God is the One who provides for us, and he does so 'richly' rather than sparingly, and for our enjoyment, not just our continued existence. That's a very positive view of money and possessions – they are from God for us to enjoy our lives. So we don't despise them or say they are meaningless. But we do know that they are not what life is really all about.

Paul is not simply saying that there's more to life than money. Even our culture often manages to work that out. He's going further and saying life isn't about money *at all*.

Picture a runner in a marathon. At various points along the race, people hand out drinks for the runners, who gulp them down and then press on. Imagine one particular runner starting to think that these drinks are great. He collects as many as he can. He's still running, but he's clutching lots of drink bottles in his arms. He slows down because he's trying to carry so many, and eventually he stops running altogether.

What might someone say to him? You'd say, at the very least, that he'd lost the point of the race! The race isn't about collecting the drinks; they are just helpful along the way. Likewise, life isn't about money and possessions; these are just aids on the way through.

The person who understands this will then be 'rich in good deeds', 'generous' and 'willing to share' (1 Timothy 6:18). This truly rich person will hand around their drinks, because they know life isn't about collecting these. They will give to others, because their hope is in God, who has given richly to that person.

In so doing, says Paul, the rich person will lay up treasure for himself and 'take hold of the life that is truly life' (verse 19). This is the same as Jesus telling us to lay up 'treasures in heaven' (Matthew 6:20). If we know that the point of life isn't about money but about knowing God, then our treasure will be somewhere else and of a different sort.

So, godliness with contentment is *great gain* (1 Timothy 6:6), a great way to live. It recognizes what life is about. It is more bothered about 'godliness' – knowing God and living for him – than how much we have. It isn't constantly looking for more.

It all comes down to what we think life is all about. Is it about comforts and pleasures now, or is it about godliness and relationship with God? How you answer that question will determine how you live, and whether or not you are content.

There are lots of measures of quality of life all around us. They usually appear in surveys that tell us how the quality of life has gone up, or how one country compares to another. They examine things like size of income, number of bedrooms, value of cars, and so on. But Jesus and Paul are saying that true quality of life is not measured by these things. Truly quality life – great gain – comes through living out our relationship with God, content with what we have.

Do you believe that? What do you think holds the greatest 'gain' in life? What do you think is the very best way to live? Is it having more stuff, or godliness with contentment?

The danger for Christians is that while we know the truths of the gospel, our hearts can be just as discontented as those of our non-Christian friends, neighbours and colleagues. While we sing and celebrate the gospel, our hearts long for more stuff. While we speak about serving God, we are actually serving money. Imagine:

- being happy with whatever make and age of car you have
- being content with your house just as it is
- being satisfied with your income
- being glad with the clothes you currently own
- having a heart that doesn't long for more
- not being envious of others around you
- being able to share willingly and generously

Being content is no hardship! It is contentment, after all. But we desperately need to grow in this heart attitude.

Contentment and the gospel

How, then, will the gospel teach us to have hearts that are content?

The gospel teaches us what life is all about.

Consider God's plan from creation to new creation, centring on Jesus' life, death and resurrection. The whole gospel message screams at us: life is about relationship with God. It is our standing with him that ranks high above everything else. God has worked wonderfully and sacrificially through Jesus to restore us to him. He has taken us from being hostile enemies to adopted children. He has promised a future where we will live with him. That is really what life is all about.

Being content is no hardship! It is contentment, after all.

The gospel teaches us that our biggest problem is not shortage of possessions, but our sin and God's judgment (1 Thessalonians 1:9–10). It shows us that our happiness does not lie in more money – it is in the fullness of life that Jesus brings (John 10:10). The gospel shows us a way to 'take hold of the life that is truly life' (1 Timothy 6:19).

If we reflect on the gospel and apply it to our hearts, we will indeed learn that godliness with contentment is great gain. Come back to the illustration of the marathon runner who's tempted to collect drinks rather than run the race. The point is that we're tempted to think life is all about collecting drinks, whereas the gospel focuses on the race and points us towards the finishing line. The gospel reorientates us so that we see what life is truly about, and what real life is.

Time reflecting on the gospel should leave me with a greater contentment because I have a clearer purpose to life, and because my heart is assigning 'things' their right value.

I think of James, whom I knew in my hall of residence at university. He and I did some Bible studies together and, wonderfully, he came to trust in Jesus. Not long after that, he was interviewed at our church about his journey to faith. That was many years ago now, but I can still remember some of his answers. The interviewer asked him what he had thought life was all about before he became a Christian. James spoke about his ambition of making it in life, of being successful, and a big part of that involved being rich. Then he was asked how becoming a Christian had changed that. Very simply, he replied, 'Now I know I'm rich already.'

His view had changed. He knew that God had made him rich in the most important ways, and so he was content.

Contentment in practice

Let's finish with a few thoughts on how we might combat our desire for more and cultivate contentment. We've seen that we must reflect on the gospel. But what does that look like in detail?

Firstly, *know yourself*. Get to know what you personally think will bring you contentment. That will show you what you think life is all about, and help you to apply the gospel. For some people, it's all about their house. It's building that extension, enjoying that nice furniture or putting in that new kitchen, For others it's possessions: a certain car, a larger TV, more music downloads.. For others, it's about the bank balance. It might be worth asking someone else where they think you are looking for contentment. Ask your spouse, your housemate or a friend.

Whatever it is, it should show you what you think life is really about and where you'll need to fight for contentment. If the house is your downfall, then maybe reading the IKEA catalogue isn't such a good idea. That will only cultivate a desire for more. If it's all about the latest techno-toy, then wandering round the Apple store is foolish!

What's more, we can apply the gospel specifically to our desires for more. You can say to yourself, 'Remember that a house is just a house. It's useful, and great as I pass through life, but it's not what life is all about.' You can say to yourself, 'Remember that a car is just a car. It's really helpful to get around in, and can even be fun to drive, but it's not what I'm to live for.'

Secondly, *cultivate thankfulness*. We looked at thankfulness earlier, but it's worth bringing in here, because contentment and thankfulness are such close relatives. If you are thankful for what you have, then you don't long for what you don't have. Thankfulness undercuts the desire for more. So, remind yourself of the spiritual riches we've been given in Jesus. As you begin the day, give thanks to God for what he has given you. As you feel the desire for more of something, remind yourself what you do have.

Lastly, *change your desires*. Paul writes to Timothy directly,

> But you, man of God, flee from all this, and pursue righteousness, godliness, faith, love, endurance and gentleness.
> (1 Timothy 6:11)

This comes straight after Paul's warning about the love of money. He's saying, instead of that pursuit of money and possessions, Timothy should give himself to something else. He should pursue righteousness, godliness, faith and more. It's a different agenda. Timothy should say to himself, 'This is what life is about; this is what's important.' He should think, *If I am to be discontented with my life, it should be over a lack of this, not a lack of designer clothes.*

So, we must combat the messages of the world. As we watch adverts, we'll need to say, 'Run away from wanting that stuff!' Life is about our relationship with God, so what we really need is righteousness, godliness and faith, not a new sofa.

We will need to say to ourselves that godliness with contentment is much greater gain than whatever we are being offered elsewhere.

9
hope

'Just as man cannot live without dreams, he cannot live without hope.'[1]

Those words are from a survivor of the Holocaust, Elie Wiesel, who had been in Auschwitz. He writes poignantly about the inconceivable evil of the concentration camps: the hunger, the torture, the randomness of death. He says, 'Life in this accursed universe was so distorted, so unnatural that a new species had evolved. Waking among the dead, one wondered if one were still alive.'

I cannot imagine such an experience. Yet everyone knows something of despair. The Nazi concentration camps were close to an ultimate expression of evil, but evil still exists in our world today. Tragedies still happen. We have many reasons to be sad. Tears still flow.

Wiesel says that we cannot live without hope. That's not actually true, of course. You can live without hope, but it's a miserable existence, a life dominated by despair. And some people do feel utterly hopeless. That might show itself in depression, or at worst in suicide. It can be less obvious, in being cynical or apathetic about life.

But Wiesel still has a point. If we are to live with any sense of purpose or conviction, we do need hope. We will all experience the brokenness and wrongness of the world. If we're not to give in to despair, then we need to have hope.

The big question is: what do we hope for?

Wiesel hopes for a better world. He hopes that people will learn from the evils of the past, so as not to repeat them. But he recognizes that the terrible atrocities in the world since World War 2 mean that we've not learned very well.

Other people put their hope in politicians. I still remember when the Labour Party came to power in 1997, and there was a great sense of hope. It was after a long spell of Conservative government, and many people were optimistic. I was too. In fact, as a friend and I sat watching the election results, we finally brought out the cigars and smiled. But the smiles didn't last long. In the USA, there was a great sense of hope when Barack Obama was elected President in 2008. He campaigned under the key words 'hope' and 'change'. But change was hard, and hope soon faded. Overall, we've learned to be pretty cynical about investing our hope in politicians.

Most people's hopes operate on the personal level. I know individuals who are hopeful about their career, a new relationship, a house move, a new routine or even a holiday. Will one of those things make life better in some way? They hope so.

What about Christians? We can so easily drift along with our culture. If life is hard for us, then we too can drift into feeling hopeless. Or we might be hopeful, but only hopeful about the same things as those around us.

But throughout the Bible, God teaches us that hope is a key heart attitude that his people should possess.

Trust for the future

Here's a verse that helps explain what hope is:

> . . . in order that we, who were the first to put our hope in Christ, might be for the praise of his glory.
> (Ephesians 1:12)

The apostle Paul is talking here about those who 'put our hope in Christ'. That's *trusting* Christ for something. If I put my hope in a friend to help me, then I'm trusting them to provide that help. If I put my hope in a life jacket to save me, then I'm trusting myself to its buoyancy.

Hope is faith looking forward.

So, hope is almost identical to trust, but there is a simple difference. Hope looks forward. It trusts God for something in the future, something that will happen or will be true, something you do not have here and now. So, when we look at hope in the Bible, we see that it keeps company with others words like *waiting*, *patient* or *expecting*. Hope is faith looking forward.

We sometimes make promises to one of our kids about a birthday. I might tell them what we will do, where we will go, what present they might receive. Assuming they believe me, they will be hopeful. They trust me for that future, and as a result, they wait, looking forward, expecting certain things to happen. So, hope is tied up with the person making promises for the future, and it's tied up with trusting that person.

Biblically then, hope is faith looking forward to what God has promised about the future. As a result, we find verses like these:

> Israel, put your hope in the LORD,
>> for with the LORD is unfailing love.
> (Psalm 130:7)

The people are told to put their hope in God. Why? Because with him is unfailing love. God won't ever let you down; he is worth trusting for the future, because he will never stop loving you.

> My soul faints with longing for your salvation,
>> but I have put my hope in your word.
> (Psalm 119:81)

Here is someone who's desperate for rescue. It's as if they almost can't hold on any more. But, they say, 'I have put my hope in your Word. I will trust what you have said.'

See how hope works? Hope flows from God's promises for the future and is based on God's trustworthiness to keep those promises.

Hope within this life

Hope shows itself in a variety of ways. First there is hope within this life. Hope that God will help us in difficult times, rescue us from trouble, always be with us, be working for our good in every situation, and more. You can see that sense of hope for future moments in the following verses:

> He has delivered us from such a deadly peril, and he will deliver us again. On him we have set our hope that he will continue to deliver us.
> (2 Corinthians 1:10)

> I eagerly expect and hope that I will in no way be ashamed,
> but will have sufficient courage so that now as always

Christ will be exalted in my body, whether by life or by
death.
(Philippians 1:20)

The widow who is really in need and left all alone puts her hope in
God and continues night and day to pray and to ask God for help.
(1 Timothy 5:5)

Command those who are rich in this present world not to be
arrogant nor to put their hope in wealth, which is so uncertain,
but to put their hope in God, who richly provides us with
everything for our enjoyment.
(1 Timothy 6:17)

Having hope within life now is linked to the heart attitudes we
looked at earlier, especially that of peace. I do not know what
the future holds, but I do trust God. That means I place my hope
in him, and can know his peace. We see that link in some psalms:

Yes, my soul, find rest in God;
   my hope comes from him.
Truly he is my rock and my salvation;
   he is my fortress, I shall not be shaken.
(Psalm 62:5–6)

David expresses his confidence in God as his rock and salvation.
That means God is his source of hope, and he can find rest
in him.

This hope is both because of God's specific promises, but
mainly because of God's character. He is the One who is
committed to his people, and so we can trust him. Look
at the relationship between trust and awareness of God's
unfailing love:

We wait in hope for the LORD;
    he is our help and our shield.
In him our hearts rejoice,
    for we trust in his holy name.
May your unfailing love be with us, LORD,
    even as we put our hope in you.
(Psalm 33:20–22)

It is because we know God to be like this that we can live with hope in this life now.

Hope for new life

Although we can and should have hope in life now, the main focus in the Bible is on hope for the *ultimate future* that God promises. He has said that one day, history as we know it will end, and his plans will be fulfilled. This will be the new creation. Perhaps the most wonderful description of it comes in Revelation:

> And I heard a loud voice from the throne saying, 'Look! God's dwelling-place is now among the people, and he will dwell with them. They will be his people, and God himself will be with them and be their God. "He will wipe every tear from their eyes. There will be no more death" or mourning or crying or pain, for the old order of things has passed away.'
>
> He who was seated on the throne said, 'I am making everything new!' Then he said, 'Write this down, for these words are trustworthy and true.'
> (Revelation 21:3–5)

The new creation God promises does not involve floating on clouds or playing harps. It is a recreated world where everything is as it is supposed to be. God is fully and wonderfully present.

There will be no more tears, because there will be nothing to cry over any more. As a friend of mine says to his children, it is the place where 'nothing is sad and nothing is bad'.

Those words from Revelation come at the very end of the Bible, but the promise has been there all the way through. In fact, the words above quote parts of the Old Testament where God promised this to his people (read Isaiah 25:6–9). God has constantly promised to make the world right again, and his people have been constantly called to live with that hope.

So Peter expresses it like this:

> But in keeping with his promise we are looking forward to a new heaven and a new earth, where righteousness dwells.
> (2 Peter 3:13)

What a wonderful picture – a place where 'righteousness dwells', or the home of righteousness, the place where everything is as it is meant to be.

To put it another way:

> . . . here we do not have an enduring city, but we are looking for the city that is to come.
> (Hebrews 13:14)

We're hoping for a more permanent place to live. A city that endures.

Hope and the gospel

This is where we have to see that hope is part of the gospel message. It is not that the gospel is about forgiveness now, and then God adds an extra bit about the future. His promises in the gospel are future-orientated and include the new creation.

This is why Paul describes the conversion of the Christians in Thessalonica like this:

> They tell how you turned to God from idols to serve the living and true God, and to wait for his Son from heaven, whom he raised from the dead – Jesus, who rescues us from the coming wrath.
>
> (1 Thessalonians 1:9–10)

Do you see how believing the gospel means starting to wait? The Thessalonians turned to God and trusted his promises, and on that day they started waiting for the day when Jesus comes back. Believing the gospel means trusting God for the future, having hope that we will be rescued from his wrath to come.

This is why Paul describes the gospel to the Colossian believers like this:

> To them God has chosen to make known among the Gentiles the glorious riches of this mystery, which is Christ in you, the hope of glory.
>
> (Colossians 1:27)

Paul is describing the glorious riches of the gospel message. He divides it into two parts. Firstly there is 'Christ in you'. That's now. When we respond to the gospel, we have a relationship with Jesus; we're united with him. That brings new life now, forgiveness now, adoption now, freedom now.

 But secondly, Christ in you now also brings 'the hope of glory' – that is, hope for everything that God will do in the future, because his plans are only partway through. We live now with the hope of glory. This is why Paul spoke a few verses earlier of 'the hope held out in the gospel' (Colossians 1:23).

So, hope is part of the gospel package:

> For in this hope we were saved. But hope that is seen is no hope
> at all. Who hopes for what they already have? But if we hope for
> what we do not yet have, we wait for it patiently.
> (Romans 8:24–25)

Paul asks, 'Who hopes for what they already have?' The answer
is: 'No-one'. On Boxing Day, no-one says, 'I'm really looking
forward to my presents.' After all, they've opened their
presents already (unless they have some really weird Christmas
traditions). You don't hope for something you already have.
Hope is for what you *don't* yet have.

Paul's point is that we don't have everything yet. The
Christian life looks forward to the presents God has promised
which we haven't yet opened. God has promised a day when
salvation will be complete, when we and this whole creation
will be renewed, when we will be with God, when the glory
of God will cover the world. Hope is part of the gospel
message because the gospel is not just a message about now.

Sometimes the gospel message has been reduced to trusting
Jesus and so getting a ticket to heaven. The gospel is presented
as *all* about the future. But that's clearly not the true gospel,
which is about life now, not just after death. The gospel means
we have Christ in us now, and so we live differently now.

But a more common error today is to make the gospel *all*
about life now. So when you hear the gospel presented, it may
be *only* about the difference Jesus will make to you today. You
are called to believe in Jesus because life will be better now,
you will be more fulfilled now, you will have greater purpose
now. But that's not the true gospel either. It has stopped being
a message of hope for the future. The apostle Paul wrote, 'If
only for this life we have hope in Christ, we are of all people

most to be pitied' (1 Corinthians 15:19). We have a change of life now *and* hope for the life to come. So the true gospel is 'Christ in you' now, and 'the hope of glory' in the future.

Being characterized by hope

Paul said in Romans 8, 'If we hope for what we do not yet have, we wait for it patiently' (Romans 8:25). Christians are therefore characterized by waiting, because the gospel is characterized by hope. Similarly, Peter said, 'In keeping with his promise we are looking forward . . .' (2 Peter 3:13). Christians are also characterized by looking forward, because the gospel is characterized by God's future promise. A Christian who doesn't have hope hasn't understood the gospel.

The psalms in the Old Testament display a constant awareness of hope:

> We wait in hope for the LORD;
>   he is our help and our shield.
> (Psalm 33:20)

> May your unfailing love be with us, LORD,
>   even as we put our hope in you.
> (Psalm 33:22)

> But now, Lord, what do I look for?
>   My hope is in you.
> (Psalm 39:7)

> Why, my soul, are you downcast?
>   Why so disturbed within me?
> Put your hope in God,
>   for I will yet praise him,
>   my Saviour and my God.
> (Psalm 43:5)

For what you have done I will always praise you
    in the presence of your faithful people.
And I will hope in your name,
    for your name is good.
(Psalm 52:9)

Yes, my soul, find rest in God;
    my hope comes from him.
(Psalm 62:5)

As for me, I shall always have hope;
    I will praise you more and more.
(Psalm 71:14)

I rise before dawn and cry for help;
    I have put my hope in your word.
(Psalm 119:147)

I wait for the LORD, my whole being waits,
    and in his word I put my hope.
(Psalm 130:5)

God's people are hopeful. Situations can be terrible and life can be hard, but they look to God. They remind themselves of his character (that he is loving) and his Word (what he has promised), and they are filled with hope.

This means that Christians should be realistic optimists! We are very realistic about the state of the world now. We know evil will have its day; we know there will be plenty to cry over; but we also know it will not last. I think of Jane, who lost a baby recently. It was, and is, a terribly sad situation. She and her husband have been devastated, and the experience has brought questions and doubts. But throughout, Jane has kept her eyes on her future hope. She knows that God is good and she can trust him. She wrote a note to friends recently: 'I'm missing my little girl, and waiting for Jesus to make everything right.' There is right sadness here, and a right hope.

So, we have to ask the question: are we any more hopeful than our non-Christian friends? Do our hopes revolve around different things from theirs? Do we look forward in a way that they don't? Unfortunately, we all too easily look the same as them. I think the main reason for this is that God's promises for the future can seem too remote, too distant and too unreal.

The sad fact is that our future hope often only becomes more of a reality to us when life is hard. It is when Christians have been persecuted that they've lifted their eyes to Jesus' return. It's when tears are streaming down our face that we long for the day when God will wipe them away. It's when this creation feels rubbish that we long for a new one. But when life is smooth, we too easily forget to look ahead. So many people will testify that hard times – while no-one denies that they are very tough – have served to teach them to lift their gaze and live with hope. That's what Paul says will happen:

> Not only so, but we also glory in our sufferings, because we know that suffering produces perseverance; perseverance, character; and character, hope.
> (Romans 5:3–4)

So, Christians are to be characterized by hope. Having that heart attitude changes everything. Firstly, it means simply that we keep going. The whole point of hope is that life is hard and you want it to get better. Paul speaks about the 'endurance inspired by hope' (1 Thessalonians 1:3). If we have hope, we will look through difficult times to the future that

God has promised. We shall persevere in hardships, knowing it is worth it. We shall accept old age, illness and infirmity, not lightly, but in hopeful expectation of renewed bodies. We shall face persecution or suffering, knowing justice will come. The author of the letter to the Hebrews urges his readers to keep going, and so he speaks repeatedly about their hope:

> We have this hope as an anchor for the soul, firm and secure.
> (Hebrews 6:19)

Secondly, hope changes our attitude to death: our own and that of other believers. Paul writes to the Thessalonians:

> Brothers and sisters, we do not want you to be uninformed about those who sleep in death, so that you do not grieve like the rest of mankind, who have no hope.
> (1 Thessalonians 4:13)

We are not uninformed about our hope, and so we grieve differently – we know there is a future to look forward to with our departed brothers and sisters.

Thirdly, having hearts full of hope means that we will live for God and grow in holiness. John writes, 'All who have this hope in him purify themselves, just as he is pure' (1 John 3:3). We know where God is taking this world, a place where his righteousness dwells, so we live in accordance with that new world now.

Fourthly, our hope means that even when life is good, we will still look to the future, knowing the best is yet to come (1 Timothy 6:17–19). Our hope of salvation is a 'helmet', which will protect us and keep us going (1 Thessalonians 5:8). Our hope means that we shall call out, 'Come, Lord Jesus' (Revelation 22:20). We shall be characterized by hope.

Growing in hope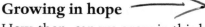

How, then, can we grow in this heart attitude?

Firstly, we must *direct our hearts* to this hope:

> Israel, put your hope in the LORD,
>   for with the LORD is unfailing love
>   and with him is full redemption.
> (Psalm 130:7)

Notice the command: put your hope in God! We have a choice as to where we place our hope. We can direct our hearts as to what we look to and rely on, where we put our expectations and confidence. This verse tells us to direct our hearts to hope in God. And it tells us why: because with him is unfailing love and full redemption. If we put our hope in a God like that, we'll never be disappointed.

It's important to know that this encouragement to hope in God is not given by someone who's finding life easy. Earlier in the psalm, this person speaks about crying out to God, waiting for God to do something for him. He's been telling himself to trust in God, and in the verse above, he widens that out and tells everyone else to hope in God as well. This isn't an encouragement from an armchair, but from the trenches.

Peter says something similar to his readers:

> . . . set your hope on the grace to be brought to you when Jesus Christ is revealed.
> (1 Peter 1:13)

We can set our hope on that day to come. We can place our hope on the grace or the kindness that God will show us on that day. Peter has already said that, in his mercy, God has given us new birth into a 'living hope' (1 Peter 1:3). But he knows that his readers could lose focus, forget, or start to hope in other things. So he tells them to direct their hearts to hope fully in God.

When it comes to hope, just as with all the other heart attitudes we've looked at, we have choices to make. It's not simply that some of us are optimists and some are pessimists. We should not simply accept whatever level of hope we feel or don't feel. We can choose whose promises we will believe and who we will trust for the future. We can choose whether to have hope, and where to place that hope.

Secondly, we grow in hope by *reflecting on God's promises*. Speaking personally, I enjoy holidays very much. As I write, I have one booked to start in a week's time, and I'm looking forward to it a lot. The reason I'm anticipating it so much is because I have a mental picture of what's involved. I don't know everything that we'll do, but I can see myself sleeping in, eating nice food, reading, walking and more.

The content of my holiday fuels my hope. It's the same with our Christian hope, for our hope turns on what God has promised for the future. In fact, without any content, it's pretty tricky to generate much hope at all. So a big problem for us is that our grasp on God's promises for the future are often vague and uncertain.

This means we need to reflect on what God has promised, fill out the content and fuel our hope. Richard Baxter was a sixteenth-century minister who once was so extremely ill that he thought he would die. As he lay in bed for months on end, he reflected on our hope for the future. He eventually recovered, and those thoughts became the basis for his first book, *The Saints' Everlasting Rest*.

Baxter said that for the rest of his life, he reflected on our future life with God every day. Towards the end of his book, he encourages his readers to reflect on the future as he did:

I hope you will value this heavenly life, and take one walk every day in the New Jerusalem . . . O try this life of meditation on your heavenly rest . . .[2]

We need to walk each day in the New Jerusalem. One way I try to do this is by learning and reflecting on key verses. I can tell myself that I am 'looking forward to a new heaven and a new earth, where righteousness dwells' (2 Peter 3:13). I can think of a time when 'there will be no more death or mourning or crying or pain, for the old order of things has passed away' (Revelation 21:4). I can mull on the time when

We need to walk each day in the New Jerusalem.

'they are before the throne of God
    and serve him day and night in his temple;
and he who sits on the throne
    will shelter them with his presence.
"Never again will they hunger;
    never again will they thirst.
The sun will not beat down on them,"
    nor any scorching heat.
For the Lamb at the centre of the throne
    will be their shepherd;
"he will lead them to springs of living water."
    "And God will wipe away every tear from their eyes." '
(Revelation 7:15–17)

③ Take time to reflect on our hope today.

Thirdly, we should *pray for hope*. Again, as with all the other heart attitudes, we must ask for God's help in this. Paul tells us that his prayers for Christians often include this element. For example:

> I pray that the eyes of your heart may be enlightened in order that you may know the hope to which he has called you, the riches of his glorious inheritance in his holy people . . .
> (Ephesians 1:18)

Paul prays that we'll know the content of our hope, that we'll see it more clearly. We live by faith and not by sight, and these are spiritual realities which we need God's help to see. As you reflect on God's promises, ask for his help to see and know this hope.

Paul also prays for people to be filled with hope:

> May the God of hope fill you with all joy and peace as you trust in him, so that you may overflow with hope by the power of the Holy Spirit.
> (Romans 15:13)

God fills us with joy and peace about what he has done, so that we overflow with hope for the future. Isn't that a great picture? Imagine overflowing with hope, being so full of it that it pours out of us.

But we shall only overflow with hope by the power of the Holy Spirit. It is as we trust him, but it is by his power; we cannot do this by ourselves. With God's help, we will live in this world differently, because we have a firm and certain hope for the next one.

conclusion

I began by saying how important our heart attitudes are. It is not enough that we know the truth about God – that truth must also shape our hearts. It is not enough that we do the right thing – right actions must flow from right hearts.

I pray that you will grow in knowledge of God and in living for God. But I also pray that you will grow in love, fear, joy, peace, humility, confidence, thankfulness, contentment and hope. These all flow from the truth of the gospel, and they all flow out into the life of discipleship to which God calls us.

We will battle to have such heart attitudes for the rest of our life. The world, the flesh and the devil are set against us. But keep going. Keep returning to the gospel, let it shape your heart. Let God do his open-heart surgery in you. It isn't easy, but it's worth it.

One day, that work will be finished. We won't ever have to remind ourselves of the truth, or tell ourselves how to think, because we will see God and the Lord Jesus with our own eyes. On that day we won't need to fight the sinful attitudes of our hearts any longer because all sin will be washed away. On that day our hearts will be perfected and all we feel shall be right and true. Look forward to that day.

notes

Introduction: welcome to heart surgery

1. Isaac Watts, *The Works of Isaac Watts. Revised and corrected by D. Jennings and P. Doddridge* (London: T. and T. Longman, and J. Buckland; J. Oswald; J. Waugh; and J. Ward, 1753), 'Love of God', Vol. 2, p. 640.

Chapter 1: Love

1. Augustine, *Homily Seven on the First Epistle of John*, available at http://www.ccel.org/ccel/schaff/npnf107.toc.html.
2. John Owen, *Communion with God*, abridged by R. J. K. Law (Edinburgh: Banner of Truth, 1991), pp. 16–17.
3. John Stott, *What Christ Thinks of the Church: Revelation 1 – 3 Expounded* (Oxford: Candle Books, 1990), p. 27.

Chapter 3: Joy

1. Timothy Keller, *Counterfeit Gods: When the Empty Promises of Love, Money and Power Let You Down* (London: Hodder & Stoughton, 2009), p. 173.
2. Edward T. Welch, *Depression: Looking up from the Stubborn Darkness* (Greensboro, NC: New Growth Press, 2004), p. 31.
3. Matthew Henry, *Commentary on the Whole Bible* (http://www.ccel.org/ccel/henry/mhc.i.html) (1707), Nehemiah, Chapter 8.

4. Joni Eareckson Tada, *Glorious Intruder: God's Presence in Life's Chaos* (Colorado Springs: Multnomah, 1989), p. 48.

Chapter 4: Peace

1. Edward T. Welch, *Running Scared: Fear, Worry, and the God of Rest* (Greensboro, NC: New Growth Press, 2007), p. 163.
2. Thomas R. Schreiner, *The New American Commentary, Vol. 37, 1, 2 Peter, Jude* (Nashville, TN: Broadman & Holman, 2003), p. 241.

Chapter 5: Humility

1. John Stott, 'Pride, Humility and God', in J. I. Packer and Loren Wilkinson (eds.), *Alive to God: Studies in Spirituality* (Downers Grove: InterVarsity Press, 1992), p. 119.
2. Ibid., p. 111.
3. Richard Baxter, *The Reformed Pastor* (Edinburgh: Banner of Truth, 1974), Chapter 3, Section 1.
4. Ibid.

Chapter 7: Thankfulness

1. Various forms of this traditional prayer appear in Anglican prayer books and elsewhere.

Chapter 9: Hope

1. Elie Wiesel, *Hope, Despair and Memory, Nobel Lecture* (1986).
2. Richard Baxter, 'The Saints' Everlasting Rest', in *The Practical Works of Richard Baxter* (Grand Rapids, MI: Baker Book House, 1981), p. 121.